The Poetry of Perestroika

Edited by
Peter Mortimer and S.J. Litherland

Translated by
Carol Rumens and Richard McKane

Other Translators
Yurij Drobyshev
Michael Molnar
Peter France
Helen Szamuely
Tim Pike
Nik Abu-Haidar
Rachel Croft
Avril Pyman

IRON
PRESS

First published 1991 by IRON Press
5 Marden Terrace, Cullercoats
North Shields, Tyne & Wear NE30 4PD, UK
Tel: 091–253 1901

Typeset by Roger Booth Associates
10 Bigg Market, Newcastle upon Tyne
in Times Medium 10.5 point

Printed by Tyneside Free Press Workshop
5 Charlotte Square, Newcastle upon Tyne

Edited by Peter Mortimer & S.J. Litherland

ISBN 0 906228 35 2

IRON Press books are represented by:
Password Books Ltd
23 New Mount Street
Manchester M4 4DE
Tel: 061–953 4009

ACKNOWLEDGEMENTS

The task of collecting and selecting recent Russian poetry proved an awesome one, and could not possibly have been done without the active co-operation and goodwill of a number of people and organisations. We would like to thank the following:

Ekaterina Shevelyova of the Soviet Writers' Union, our source for the 'official' writers; Carol Rumens and Yurij Drobyshev for hunting through recent Soviet literary magazines, and for their help in tracking down elusive biographies; Richard McKane for his contacts in the emigré world and samizdat poets in the Soviet Union; Ellena Voinoyva of Moscow who introduced us to the *People of the Night* poets and sent us many avant-garde manuscripts; the ICA in London where we heard and met the new Almanac group of performance poets during the 1988 season celebrating 'unofficial' Soviet arts; Katya Young who helped organise the Soviet Arts New Beginnings in Glasgow, 1989, inviting a batch of alternative and unofficial writers.

Thanks are also due to Mr Le Fleming and Dr Sokolov (Avril Pyman) of Durham University Russian Department for their advice, Durham University final year Russian degree students, Nik Abu-Haidar, Rachel Croft and Tim Pike, who helped us copy-taste manuscripts and worked on final translations with Carol Rumens. Both Tim Pike and Nik Abu-Haidar acted as vital couriers for IRON Press during 1990 Moscow visits. Yurij Drobyshev again for the huge amount of invaluable time he gave assisting Carol Rumens in translation.

Thanks to Jenny Attala, former Literary Officer of Northern Arts, for her encouragement and belief in the project; to Peter France of Edinburgh University – for many years a translator of banned poets; Carl Patten and Nigel Culverwell for helping hunt down a cover poster; Susan Causey, Manchester's Olympic Festival Exhibitions Organiser, for her help in arranging permission for Sergei Mosienko's cover poster, which formed part of The Cornerhouse, Manchester's 1990 *Posters of Perestroika* exhibition; Rachel Levitas and Chris Nurse likewise for cover-hunting at various Russian art exhibitions in London galleries; Antonia Byatt of the Arts Council for helping steer us through difficult times; translator Michael Molnar for putting us on to the work of the Leningrad poets; Connie Booth for endless patience in typesetting Russian names; Alla Smith of Whitley Bay for last minute biographical translations; Bloodaxe Books for their support.

Carol Rumens was Northern Arts Literary Fellow at Durham and Newcastle Universities 1988–90.

S.J. Litherland's visit to the Soviet Union in 1987 was financially assisted by a Northern Arts Travel Award.

An earlier version of Olga Sedakova's poem *A Chinese Journey* was first published in *Index on Censorship,* March 1990.

Gennady Aygi's poems were first published in this English translation in *Chapman* magazine and *Temenos 10.*

– *The Editors*
November 1990

CONTENTS

(Translators in italics)

FOREWORD

Although this book has a topical title, its roots, for my part, can be traced back to the mid-seventies, when I was lucky enough to be invited on a writers' visit to the Soviet Union.

This visit was due mainly to the efforts of the Newcastle teacher and poet Alan Brown, indefatigable in his fostering of East–West cultural relationships. Brownie got me on the writers' delegation, and I soon realised that the great lumbering behemoth of the USSR fascinated me. It was to be the first of three visits in little more than a decade, and each time I felt I came to understand the country more.

It seemed almost a mirror-image of the USA, which has a glittering, seductive exterior often disguising an emptiness within. Not much to excite on the outside in the Soviet Union, but once the layers are peeled back, they reveal a highly complex (sometimes infuriating) people.

I also found myself fascinated by the part played by the nation's poetry. As an editor of a small press in England, I was fully accustomed to poetry being marginalised, an irrelevancy to the vast proportion of the population. In the USSR poetry was a natural part of life. Poetry magazines sold in their hundreds of thousands, where here, if lucky, they sold in their hundreds. Often an edition would sell out on the day of issue. Instead of being neglected, poets were considered important. Many were supported.

I also came to realise that much of the poetry was turgid, hack, conservative, non-imaginative, churned out by cosy Writers' Union members with more of an eye for the easy life than the creative turmoil. The irony then: in one country a relatively adventurous poetry which no-one read, in the other, a highly traditional form eagerly devoured by the populace.

But what was also growing was the Moscow–Tyneside connection, and the Russian writer and singer Ekaterina Shevelyova expressed an interest in publishing a Russian book of contemporary Northern English poetry. This eventually led in '88 to the book *Poets of Northern England* (Raduga), an extensive 200 page anthology of 23 poets, ironically the biggest collection of modern Northern poetry anyone has published anywhere. The poets were also delightfully surprised to find themselves paid generously in sterling. The first edition sold out rapidly in the USSR, and all the poets over here have reason to thank Ekaterina Shevelyova for her dedication in seeing the project through.

It was this book, plus the Soviet visit in '87, when fellow writer Jackie Litherland and I felt the stirrings of perestroika and glasnost, that really got our own edition going. During this visit, we realised the old order was beginning to change; for the first time we got to see alternative poets and artists, bringing out their own

9

books, or staging their own avant-garde exhibitions in tower-block basements.

Ekaterina Shevelyova supplied some names and, as the months progressed, we spread our net increasingly wider. Being novices, we made many mistakes.At one point we found ourselves bankrupt, having spent a great deal of translation money putting into English a whole series of poems which we discovered were dross. At this stage, the Arts Council refused funding, and the project seemed destined to be strangled at birth.

Fortunately, Durham University Russian Department (staff and students) agreed to some 'copy tasting', doing unpaid rough translations which allowed us to choose which poems deserved taking further and our translators talent-spotted for us from their own sources. The brief we set ourselves was to publish work either written in the new glasnost/perestroika era, or poetry previously written, which only now *could* be published.

The result is a mixture of new and well-known names, many different styles; from the familiar declamatory voice of Yevtushenko, through to the avant-garde 'list' poetry of Rubinshtein; from the harrowing prison poetry of Akhmetov, to the metaphysics of Aygi. It may takes years for Soviet writers to come properly to terms with the new age. Many poets who had churned out the obligatory line before, simply churned out the new party line. We didn't want them.

What we did want was a sense of real creative energy, amid all the confusion, the disasters, the arguments that have come with the transition. Such an anthology can't possibly cover the whole range of new writing in such a vast country, but we do hope it gives some flavour of how a nation's poets emerge, often blinking, into the new light.

Peter Mortimer
Co-editor

* * *

We were offered peas out of a tin and a specially baked strawberry cake. Peter Mortimer and I (and fellow poet Steve Walker) were in a Moscow high-rise flat of Vladimir Druk three years ago. He was an unknown young poet and had gathered others to meet us; all belonged to the 100-strong writers' and artists' collective 'People of the Night'. The poetry was satirical and sometimes nonsensical, an obvious counter-blast to the solemn lyrical poetry of the Writers' Union (which had a curious affinity to our pre-First World War Georgian poetry). The poets gestured, laughed a lot. Druk reminded us of our own Richard Caddel, circa 1970s, full of busy plans to retake the language.

These were early, heady days for glasnost and perestroika, economic privations hadn't emerged and changing society seemed as easy as stepping off one train onto another. A few nights later we were in the more comfortable flat of Oleg Chukhontsev, newly made poetry editor of Novy Mir, who was busy bringing in poets from the cold of a literary Siberia. Generous and hospitable, he and his wife put on a hastily improvised meal and offered us vodka laced with bright orange berries. It became a long session even by Russian standards, and we walked in the early hours under Moscow trees arguing about what we considered were their fanciful ideas of Western life. We mentioned unemployment and poverty co-existing with wealth and goods... but there was a barrier greater than language. We might as well have been Martians. There was a lot of past to confront and it was absorbing them like partners emerging from a bitter marriage. Problems of the West didn't concern them, even though those problems might become theirs.

Meeting the two writers, not of the old 'approved' school, was a high point and prompted the notion of a poetry of perestroika book. Also, we were wondering: what had happened to writers within the Writers' Union (who were hosts of our trip), both the more daring and safe, what on earth were they scribbling as all sorts of barriers came down?

Druk is now a member of the Writers' Union (although, as he tells us, in 'opposition' to it) and Chukhontsev, then sceptical of the security of his position, is still at the Novy Mir desk. Their poetry has now moved into the mainstream which has broadened to include nearly everyone like a flooding river, an extraordinary situation for the once tightly conformist literary scene. The only ones pushed to the edges might be the former party hacks and those sterling avant-gardists who will always try to say the unsayable.

We were forced to extend our original plan of having 15 poets to encompass the work brought to our attention. What *was* the poetry of perestroika? It came to mean for me poetry that was once proscribed or *would have been* under the old system and was now being published or written. This included past work such as Yevtushenko's *Letter to Yesenin*, which was suppressed and only now publishable, Akhmadulina's poem *This is Me,* written in 1968, published 1989, the bitter secret poems of Boris Slutsky who didn't live to see himself acclaimed, the terrifying prison poems of Akhmetov (in camps from the age of 17 to 38) who provides for the book raw images of suffering which other poets create symbols for, and the gentle metaphysical poems of Gennady Aygi also banned. Most of the others have been written since perestroika and glasnost began in 1985, so the present and the newly acquired past intermingle.

We also sought to represent as many different styles as possible in the belief that this was an indication of literary freedom and health, although it might offend purists in each school. What surprised us was the diversity. Years of conformity and repression seemed to have had very little effect on poetic invention (unlike

11

the devastating effect on Soviet art), which must be due to the survival of the great poetry of the early 20th century (pre and post revolution), of the circularised work of Akhmatova, Pasternak, Mandlestam and others, and the 60s' thaw breakthrough of Yevtushenko and Voznesensky. Russian poetry didn't lack leaders, what it lacked was a visible throng producing new writers. Poets had been shut away from each other, developing in isolation or small sects.

Take away restraints and barriers and what do you have? We often found mistrust, confusion and a clinging to old ways of segregation: poets of different schools refusing to rub shoulders, groupings which would not cross demarcation lines in print. But we felt the very act of publishing an anthology to include so many different names was to challenge the past's cruel exclusions. It is our contribution to literary perestroika.

Poets here fall in love like Gandlevsky, or mock wickedly the iconisation of Lenin like Kibirov, or have Puckish games with words like Druk or agonise with Dostoyevskian intensity like Voznesensky. Slutsky fumes ironically alongside the delicate philosophising of Sedakova, or the sardonic pessimism of Prigov is bedfellow to the conscience-searching documentation of Shevelyova. For me, a crucial inclusion was Brodsky's beautiful poem of exile published in a Russian magazine.

In this book the past still dominates. There are scores to settle, questions to frame. The poets ask themselves: Who is guilty? They answer: No-one. Everyone.

Jackie Litherland
Co-Editor

* * *

When the editors first mentioned to me their plans for an anthology of 'Poetry of Perestroika', I felt both enthusiastic and uneasy. What kind of an animal the Poetry of Perestroika might be, I had no clear idea, but it captured the imagination. A galloping chimaera, brilliantly coloured, firing off ideas in all directions, phantasmagoric, illimitable, comparable to the literary miracle that the 1917 revolution generated among writers in its early years? But wait a moment – 'perestroika' was less an intellectual concept than a catchphrase, its real goals, economic. Did poets really feel creatively stirred and disturbed or were they as cynical as the average Soviet-in-the-street, who has asked for bread and been given, as so often, the ideological stone in its latest hollow manifestation? Poets, after all, are usually light-years ahead, imaginatively, of the politicians. In any country, the job of the politicians (if only they knew it) is to try to catch up with the poets, not the other way round!

Glasnost, of course, was another matter, a spiritual and literal reality. But it wasn't originated by the founders of perestroika. Good poets have always had

12

their own underground streams and secret channels of glasnost. Perhaps the light of day would in fact dry up these precious streams?

Many of the first poems I looked at bore out the gloomier view. Obedient perestroika donkeys trotted obediently from their stables, with not a wonderful chimaera in sight. Russia-watchers detected a failure of nerve among creative artists. The people's appetite had been whetted for facts, information, opinions. It was journalism that now, intellectually and morally, held centre stage.

Not unpredictably, the most interesting poems of perestroika seemed to be those that were critical of it, or simply reflected the daily misery that has often been its immediate result. A poetry of half-humorous, half-anguished complaint began to emerge. Prigov's *Here I am frying a chicken* and Kuzovleva's *Woman and Perestroika* are examples. These are not poems of great artistry but they are immediately moving, authentic cries from the heart.

A good deal of religious poetry is now being written. Little I have read has captured my interest. It is probably exciting for Russian poets to feel they can now express their personal faith, but the familiar dogmas do not make for very exciting reading. There are exceptions, however: Yunna Moritz and Oleg Chukhontsev, for example, seem to me fine metaphysical poets whose linguistic inventiveness matches the intensity of their religious feeling.

Some poems written in response to the new 'permission to criticise' are not so much concerned with the present as with a re-evaluation of the past. Ekaterina Shevelyova's *Memo about 1968*, for instance, is a retrospective view of events in Czechoslovakia that could not have been published at the time, though, on evidence given in the poem itself, the poet had made some notebook jottings. Twenty years is a long gestation for a poem. How different would it have been if she had written it then? How much have these first perceptions been coloured by later political developments?

Literary perestroika has meant, above all, that poets and poems previously banned from publication are flooding into view. It was not in the scope of this book to include the great poets of the recent past who, after all, are already widely published in the West. However, an exception was made for Boris Slutsky, a fine poet, if not of the first rank (i.e. Mandelstam, Pasternak), who died in 1986 and whose work is not well known here. He effectively played the role of public, 'official' poet. Yet during the fifties he wrote a number of anti-Stalin poems, unpublished or published only in samizdat, and responded angrily to the anti-semitism of the times, so that his voice sounds fresh and relevant today.

It seems a seven-league stride from Slutsky to the young Soviet poet Vladimir Druk. Druk's work, though, is I think more suggestive than any other of how far-reaching the embryonic literary revolution may yet turn out to be. His poetry is what in the West would be called ludic. Sometimes suggestive of the 'beat' poets, and related to the lively sloganeering of the Mayakovsky/Yevtushenko school, it is refreshingly free of propaganda. Moving still farther from the didactic style to an intense, inward-looking lyricism, we find one of the most interesting of the new poets, Polina Ivanova. She has a wholly original voice, yet there is some almost-familiar, introspective Western quality to the feeling.

It is painful to envisage a Russia in which poets are as foreign to the living tradition as they are in Britain, and poetry turned into a kind of heritage-museum of 'greats'. However, it is surely too early to be pessimistic. A whole chunk of literary history is missing from the experience of Russian writers and though it is now in the process of being restored, assimilation cannot happen overnight. The young writers have a major task of reclamation ahead – the discovery not only of the lost or partly-lost generations of the past but their lost contemporaries in exile, poets such as Joseph Brodsky whose work is at last beginning to appear in the Soviet Union. Only when this task is complete will the full effects of literary perestroika be felt. Perhaps it is not too fanciful to compare the poetic imagination to a bird reared in captivity. You cannot expect that bird to fly and soar as soon as the cage is opened. So far, the poetry of perestroika represents the flexing of stiff and battered wings, the first notes of the forgotten song.

Carol Rumens
Translator

* * *

I met Tatiana Bek at the Glasgow New Beginnings readings. The poems the editors selected here are direct to the point of therapy. I think back to sessions in friends' Moscow kitchens, in June 1989. When she says, 'Oh, we cannot wait for a single day more: / give us the truth right now!' one thinks of the surge of 'glasnost' material, not flooding, but being easily absorbed by the Soviet market. There is a not-quite-Cassandra quality in the last lines: 'I would have gone mad. But who will spot / the new warning signs for them?'

One of the more defined groupings in this anthology is that of the Almanac Poets from Moscow, who performed at the ICA in London in 1988. Koval has a blend of cynicism, common to the Almanac poets, and buffoonery on the page and in performance (his poems are often sung by Andrei Lipski). If he plays the fool in his poems he does it intelligently and consciously. His poem on the rouble notes has gained value as the rouble plummets to all time lows. The Almanac poets include Eisenberg, the gentlest personality; Gandlevsky, the most lyrical; the young poet Novikov, whose poems have a flavour of the sixties; Prigov (the most well-known), a deliberately menacing, incantatory poet; and Kibirov. Timur

Kibirov has a wry-humoured treatment of Lenin's Childhood: 'how strange it all is, if one thinks about it a little.' If Kibirov can satirise iconoclastically such a consciously melodramatic subject, one wonders where his undoubted lyric-narrative talents could go. In Mikhail Eisenberg's poem we glimpse a reverence of language. His poem has a 'pre-glasnost' beginning: the poet has to pose a positive to find a negative. It was this poem that drew me into a comparison, say, of the unknown poets on the London café/pub circuit and Moscow poets: 'Oh, for how many years had we got used/ to the non-work discipline.'

I live a mile or so from Tower Bridge, and at first I thought that Cobrin would be trespassing on, for him, unfamiliar territory. Seeing the torture devices in the Tower he says, 'we know different tortures', and finishes, 'it's good that the prison became a museum'. When I visited Moscow (for the first time since my school days) at the invitation of the Soviet Writers' Union to contribute to the Akhmatova Conference in 1988, the Kremlin seemed tiny (on the analogy of the popular song 'When I was small and Christmas trees were tall'). It was only the KGB's Lubyanka that looked huge. There seems in Cobrin to be a wistfulness for his own country in these two poems. I liked the line of the Russian post-graduate, strolling through Cambridge, 'there is no medicine for immune deficiency of the conscience'.

I translated with Helen Szamuely and did readings of Nizametdin Akhmetov while he was still in psychiatric hospital under Gorbachev. Irina Ratushinskaya, like him a winner of the Rotterdam 'persecuted poet' prize, had already been released. I was struck by the brutalised honesty of these poems – part of a 40-page manuscript written before Akhmetov was transferred to a mental hospital in the 80s. He told me he dared not write there. *Siberian Birches* show that he was able to 'escape' from labour camp into a harmony with nature. But it is his poem *Back beyond*, which I include in my own readings, that establishes Akhmetov's acute psychological self-awareness, despite his terrible state. I argued with the Union of Writers' English desk officer in Moscow that he was by no means a naive poet. Soviet readers of *Yunost* have now been able to read his prose pieces including *Freedom Street*. For twenty years of his life from the age of 17, he was incarcerated, on the flimsiest of pretexts initially, as a Bashkir (a Turkic speaking minority – Akhmetov was originally from Chelyabinsk); in Tashkent he had befriended Crimean Tartars. He is now writing a novel. I believe 14 years after he wrote *Back beyond* he has the strength and anger to come together with his own self.

Richard McKane
Translator

15

BELLA AKHMADULINA

This is Me

To E.Y. and V.M. Rossels

This is me at two in the afternoon,
Held up by the midwife like a trophy.
Lutes are playing above me. Fairy-wands
Tickle me. All my soul understands
Is a flood of golden colour – this is me
On a burning day the summer before the war,
Gazing round at the beauty of existence.
With 'Snowstorms haze the sky'[1] and 'Hushabye Baby'[2],
I get into the habit of being alive.
But this, alas, is me, ruined by war,
Subject to Ufa's[3] gloomy supervision.
Winter and hospital, how white they are!
I notice I have not been called, but those
Who died instead are in the blurry face
Of the clouds. This is me, my countenance
Ugly, bluish, body just released
From torment, at the height of expectation,
Hearing something smaller than a sound.
Not until later will I value this
Habit of hearing the eternal roll-call
Of nameless things in my name-giving soul.
This is me, decked out in purple, haughty,
Young and fat. But I have trained my mouth
In the smile of a poet before death.
There is a game between word and word
That's like the trembling between heart and heart.
The only obligation is to trace it
With artless method in a flowing hand.
These words are bride and bridegroom. This is me
Who speaks, laughs. And like a village priest
Asks blessings on their secret union.
That's why the passing fairies scatter whispers

And laughter. How unlike the rest I am
With my forehead and my singer's curving neck.
I love this mark of singularity.
My handwriting races like a young hound
After distant prey. It's caught. My soul
Freezes.. This is me. I curse and cry.
Let the paper continue to be white.
It was dictated from the sky to me,
This task. I was unable to resolve it.
I put my neck to the torture of a harness.
How others weave their words I do not know.
I haven't strength, I haven't the technique.
Let me alone. A little person, this
Is me. To all who live I am a twin.
I doze while travelling by electric train,
My plain face nods off against my bag.
I've never had good fortune in excess.
Thank God it hasn't happened that I'm richer,
More honoured than my neighbours on this earth.
I'm with my weary fellow-citizens,
Flesh of their flesh. It's good. In long arrays
At shops, cinemas, stations, I stand last
In the queue for the cashier, behind the bold
Young fellow and the old woman who wears
A fleecy shawl, merged with them like a word
From my language, and a word from theirs.

1968

1. *A well known poem by Pushkin, often taught to children*
2. *Literally, 'Byushki-byu', a Russian Lullaby*
3. *Town in the Urals*

NIZAMETDIN AKHMETOV

Never

I never talk
with anyone
in fragrant lilac tones.
I knew god,
catlike looked at the King,
but I cursed heaven
and renounced earthly laws.

On your days of joy,
on your black days of grief,
I do not laugh with you,
I do not grieve with you.
I am star ash,
I am the shadow of executed words,
I do not search here for altars and truth.
I shall never
bow before
anyone
and never
lower my eyes.
I am
nothing
to anyone,
no one is sacred to me
on the summits of my anguish.
On the last journey,
in the last December
I will follow after all of you,
shot point blank.
But at no time
and for no one
has this wolf's glare
softened into a smile.

'There was a smell of sweat'

There was a smell of sweat,
foul,
of a confession
for sale,
proud and
alive,
a smell of passion,
fear,
and suffering,
a smell of a human alone.
No smell of a woman,
her scent.
No smell of anyone's youth.

1976

'Back beyond the burnt out, disfigured day'

Back beyond the burnt out, disfigured day
I don't remember myself as young.
Unpardoned by yesterday
I look my shadow in the eyes.

I glide beyond the echo of past words
into myself and deeper, as a ghost.
I follow with chill surprise
the shade of dreams I dreamed.

I go to myself as though to a friend,
a dagger behind my back.
And I have no strength, no anger
to come together with my own self.

1976

How Simple It Is

On The Death of G.P. Budaev

Living is like being on short rations,
doled out from morning to morning.
But there is no hunger, no pain in the noose.
How simple it is to die.

The prescription is just about in the bag:
and you and your TB are in the noose.
How simple it is to soap lightly
the end of a twisted rope of rags,

to move the stool near the door,
to throw with your own hand
the lasso improvised from your underpants
onto the electric light fitting.

Not very aesthetic! So what?
A million activated bacteria
toll the bell in the brain,
and it's as simple as the law.

Was it simple-minded or wise?
to decide everything so simply:
leaving behind you just your Police File
and your emaciated corpse for the bacteria.

Your insignificant corpse may go to the red bacteria
and your life to the noose of the law.
It's simple – the dead TB victim
hangs – a symbol of guilt.

How simple it is – my God how simple! –
to carry all the corpses in one's memory!
But is it entirely extravagant
to kill once for every one of them?

1977

Gennady P. Budaev hanged himself in Vladimir Prison in 1974

'Oh, Siberian birches!'

Oh, Siberian birches!
Didn't you, with a virgin's longing
straggle over the taiga
searching me out?

You got lost among the pines
in the damp fir groves,
and autumn caught you out
in tattered summer shawls.

You put necklaces
on your swan throats,
you shook out
the golden sheaves of braided hair.

Yesterday morning
you looked so frigid,
but now the goat-footed winds
are playing around with you.

Oh, the fun of the taiga,
every day is a miracle,
and the delights of the labour camp –
I know them all too well.

White-figured, gentle,
by the age-old trunks
you look like orphans
standing by the portly merchants' wives.

When the snows fall
the taiga will suddenly see
poor nuns
in severe, white clothes.

In the eternal, petrified green,
in the heat, the starlessness, the frost –
naked virginity,
the chastity of braided hair.

I would not know without you,
when around all is evergreen,
how to distinguish the silk
of Indian summer from the cotton of spring.

I wave to you as I pass
with a light sunny sadness.
A horse with a fiery mane
has been waiting for me for many years.

1979

I'm Talking to you in Russian

My soul did not seek kinship
with you, of which I am not proud.
Is that why you and I, Russia,
have found so little happiness?

Was I begotten in an alien womb?
But I succeeded, and not alone,
in getting to know Siberia,
Mordovia, Vladimir, Kolyma[1].

It was not my fate alone
on finding kinship to get prison,
to await the thunder of trouble from each storm cloud.
and be a stranger in my own home.

Between us mountains and deserts,
between us wars and centuries.
How can I call myself your son,
and stay with you for more than a day?

The bridges between us are too narrow,
the hostile tracks not yet overgrown...
I'm talking to you in Russian,
for all that is unRussian – forgive me:

forgive the memory so alive for me
of my unexterminated genes,
forgive me for not being able
to love you to the point of betrayals.

Our blood is not compatible,
our hearts reject each other,
and even while I speak and write in Russian
I am full of unRussian thoughts.

But still I know that even as non-Russians
we have to understand in Russian
that we will not release each other:
we are bound together, though we are strangers.

1978

1. *Prison Camps.*

GENNADY AYGI

Field: Jasmine in Flower

but how
can that
Foundation not be which is everywhere present for thought: like some
Skeleton not-of-the-universe! –

that like God-Presence:

being felt: is irrevocable:

how can it not be here: behind momentary fusion of-Place-and-of-Time:

and: of-our-Cordiality!–

as it is (like foundation of thoughts)
here: behind each revealed island
of white (as of a second incandescence: having outlived colour: once more
become only idea!):

at dawn how clear this Skeleton not-of-the-universe! –

it is Seen it Shines: through islands
of white: in the field: ever whiter

1971

You-Day

and reaching especially the hearts of swifts
the wind was light – bearer of gladness:

(yourself you were so much in every place!)

in shimmering-and-prayer for you
forgiving
Day
reared hugely up! –

in the swifts cried (like a child-soul):
utter-inaccessibility! –

yet in it there was openness – here
as if
from light! –

and hearing was – secretly-still... –

(keen – in you – as in the crying)

At Night: Shuddering

to A.M.

at Night, unexpectedly,
I see, shuddering, – between pillow and face – the face of buried friend:
it is – like wrapping paper (the contents removed):
features – like folds... unbearable these mutilated traces!...
grief itself unliving! – all – seems made of a thing – that is more and more
dead... –
and pain is abolished – without trace – by new pain only: its lifeless
successiveness!... –
existence – like an action? – of crumpling – as if calculated!...
'all' – like a concept? – is – like a wrapping!... in order to rustle and be
mutilated...

1971

TATIANA BEK

'Oh life, long as the telling'

Oh life, long as the telling,
short as a ballad,
wished for as a caress,
bitter as prison soup.

Oh life, I don't want to, don't need to
and will not go to court with you.
I will not fall off the tightrope,
while the trial is in progress.

Certain signs give me strength:
first, the poppies turning red
with their black-ink hearts
on the slopes of the distant wasteland;

second, the light that will not go out
in the huge doorways of childhood,
whose world torments and teases me
and makes me come in to its inheritance;

third, the family cemetery
by Vodnoy stadium,
that inexorably calls me to itself
with lilies-of-the-valley, cloudbursts and missing people;

fourth, the wind that I love,
powerful as blood in the aorta,
but light as the belongings of pilgrims –
now I'm running out of fingers;

fifth, that I will never be alone
while there are still in the world,
with their scratches and patched clothes:
the old and the children.

'A breath in and a breath out'

A breath in, and a breath out.
And to this day, carefree and bold
I cried at your requiems,
but death slept within me and never woke.

Everything has changed! Walking the narrow borderline,
I look at simple things not so much
in malevolent depression,
but with the clear eyes of one saying farewell.

I shall not go by a roundabout way,
or hide my knowledge in a haystack...
I shall make thinking about death so homely
that it shall be necessary as a lamp.

'This is the sunset of the century'

This is the sunset of the century of the bullet.
We are only half living in the light of the world.
We, big, heavy children,
live out the life of our fathers.

Oh, we cannot wait for a single day more;
give us the truth right now!
Within each of us our relatives who perished
murmur their stories that were never shouted out.

... While we argue in the dark
and crack hollow nuts
you our home country
were laid out on the hills

between the past and the future.
Not only woods and fields
are hospitable in Russian,
but also the harsh prisons,

and graves for the living,
and sick-bays for the healthy...
I would have gone mad. But who will spot
the new warning signs for them?

JOSEPH BRODSKY

From *The Victory of Memories*

1

In Memory of My Father: Australia

I dreamed you came to life again, and departed
for Australia. The voice, three-echoed, called me
and complained about the climate, the wallpaper;
the flat still hadn't been rented. *It's a pity*
it's not in the centre, but it's by the sea,
second floor, with bath, although no lift.
Your legs had swollen. "But I've left my slippers"
rang brisk and clear. Then, through the handset, suddenly
came a howling, "Adelaide, Adelaide", something
started to clatter, banged like a shutter hitting
against a wall, ready to fly off its hinges.

Nevertheless, this is better than soft ash
in a crematorium jar, and the pledged token
– these fragments of a voice, a soliloquy
and attempts to pretend unsociability

for the first time since the occasion you became smoke.

3

'Darling, today I left the house'

Darling, today I left the house late in the evening
For a breath of fresh sea-air. The sun burned low
In its gallery like a Chinese fan, and a cloud
Puffed itself up like the lid of a grand piano.

A quarter-century's passed since you were mad about dates and kebabs.
You flirted with me, sang a bit, sketched on a notepad
In inks. Then you fell for a chemical engineer,
And, to judge from your letters, became enormously stupid.

In suburban and city churches you've lately been seen
At the funerals of friends – now succeeding each other swiftly.
And I'm glad there are distances more inconceivable
In this world than the one that exists between you and me.

Don't misunderstand me, though. There is nothing connected
Now to your voice, body, name. It's not that someone destroyed them
But that, to forget one life, a man requires
One more, as a minimum. I have lived this portion.

You've been lucky, too. Where but in snaps could you always remain
Unblemished, young, merry, mocking? Time, you see, having collided
With memory, learns about powerlessness. In the shadows
I smoke, and inhale the rot of the ebb-tide.

4

To Suzanne Martin

The bees haven't flown, nor has the horseman gone off at a gallop
The new gang in the Yannikulum coffee-shop chatters
in old-fashioned argot. Ice melting in a tall glass
lets you step in the same water twice, without quenching your thirst.

Eight years have rushed by. Wars have flared up and vanished.
Families have shattered, faces have passed in newspaper-flashes,
the announcer gasped "oh my God" and aeroplanes dropped down.
Linen can still be washed, but you can't iron mortal skin.

Things harden so as to keep their place in the memory.
From the long view, though, to be born in it is less easy
than to fade, as it leaves town, moves into years, runs after
pure time, devoid of bliss and of terracotta.

Life without us is conceivable, darling, that's why
there is landscape: the bar, the hills, a cloud in clear sky
above the field of that battle where statues become
cold, and proclaim the victory of human form.

OLEG CHUKHONTSEV

'On the Kama and Bielaya rivers today'

On the Kama and Bielaya rivers today
there are woods under water and woods far away,
little islands in deserts of water,
the stream beds are drowned, and on the new sea
here bushes, there chimneys float up into view
on the Kama and Bielaya rivers.

And the rivers no longer remember their banks!
In spring from the meadowlands spruces and stacks
are swept down the tide of snow water.
On the warfront of rivers from high in the East
like corpses the water-logged logs eddy past –
they say they'll be fished from the Volga.

The waves of the war – live trees felled by the wind;
in our millions we've come through the ordeal by fire
and preserved it in annals of granite,
but now the ordeal by water is here,
waters in front of us, waters behind,
and above us the gulls shriek and vanish.

My country! Oh motherland pitted with graves
of brothers, we must be the darlings of fate
to call down the floods on our pastures
and sacrifice forests to fresh-water seas
and ourselves for the sake of the harvest-to-be
launch our corn and our bread on the waters.

All right then, we'll plough up the river's black earth,
we'll walk down drowned beds to the wide river's mouth,
and water once fresh will grow salty;
all around us, beneath us, the flow of the dark,
and over the Kama, like kopecks, the stars,
and the ozone-filled air like a tonic.

The night spreads out wide, presses down on our chests.
Stop then, and breathe in. No return to the past.
Only waves wander over the Kama.
Like a drill the boat's engine hammers its tune,
and the heart beats in time, but why and for whom?
The far side of the buoys all is darkness.

'...and in the dark'

...and in the dark I shoved the usual door –
and there was an eerie light, and a strange roar –
where had I come? – they sat around the table
and I stared wildly at them all point-blank
and started back. The lock snapped shut behind me.
And there I stood, the handle in my back.

And there they sat, and I could hear the din.
And my father came and said to me: Walk in.
The place to which you've come is always open.
You know them all. – He showed me where to sit.
– But you are dead! I said. And he reproached me:
don't speak of things that you don't know about.

He sat down, and I cast my eyes around.
Marrowfat peas oozed butter, the table groaned
with wine, fat onions and meat in aspic,
and suddenly, as my eye fell on the cakes
and honey, and the bowls of pig's foot jelly,
the thought shot through me: this is for a wake.

They sat like members of one family,
sons and their fathers of an age, and I
recognised them, with a new recognition,
and shuddered, and the glass in my hand froze:
I saw my mother sitting in the corner,
she smiled at me like a still living soul.

Her iron tureen as usual in her lap, she sat
with strangely youthful looks, in her corner seat,
smiling a private smile, but all the time more plainly
the spots showed on the skin beneath her eyes,
as if she risked having to live, and hated
the thought of stepping in the same river twice.

Mother, I said, you are not with me now,
nor all the rest, just the idea of you.
But I shall come – and you will come back, father,
beneath this light, and mother, you will come too.
– Don't speak of things you cannot know, they muttered,
you'll shudder at these things, when once you know.

And all stood up to drink a parting cup,
and I too tried to stand, but could not get up.
I tried, I tried, but then the doors flew open
as in a lift, flew open and slammed to,
upwards it rushed, or downwards, rushing somewhere
faster and faster, and tears began to flow.

And all were swallowed up. Not one remained.
I raised my eyes, but now I saw no friend,
no father, mother, not a recollection,
myself alone, and my life's singleness,
and a sharp chill ran deep through my reflections –
conscious of death or death of consciousness.

And I drew a line under the years I'd had,
dividing life into this part and that,
and entered the accounts as in a ledger.
That part of life was carefree, easy, light,
light, easy, free of care, youthful and bitter,
but I have still to live this other life.

1975

'Suddenly through the dark'

Suddenly through the dark
Comes a noise, hair-thin.
What is it? A twig's squeak?
A cricket's crisp rustling?

Whose pain is it, whose delirium?
Has a night-pilot flown past?
I need sleep, but sleep won't come.
The sound is stuck to my ears.

It's as if someone stood
With a toy sword raised at his head,
Awaiting his time to strike
Or to collect a debt.

Mother is by the window,
In the bowl there's hissing soap.
I've got to sleep. But sleep
Won't come, not a peep.

Evening, the family, the house,
Light in a thread of hair.
Nothing shames me so much
As to gulp a mouthful of air.

Whether or not it's You,
God, I've no strength for listening
Any more to this tremulous, distant
Noise of mosquito-wings.

'*I am not drawn to this freedom*'

I am not drawn to this freedom;
as years go by, what I love
more and more is not my country,
not Rus, nor the dull sky above

– though I love these too – but, glancing
over the plains, you yearn
from this land of spiritual exile
for the city that cannot be seen,

and somewhere mid-path to Izborsk[1]
or perhaps to Damascus, you'll feel
with tremulous heart, the embrace
that is poverty-stricken, blissful,

and in ultimate homesickness stand,
clutching your ash in your hand.

*1. one of the few ancient Russian towns whose
buildings survived the Bolshevik reconstruction,
situated not far from Pskov*

YURI COBRIN

Anglo-Russian Motif

Only retired British army officers
work at the Tower of London.

I

Blue Tower Bridge
spans the Thames.
The Tower spire
sparkles like a gold brooch pin.
Mr Smith is relaxing,
drinking steadily at the bar:
English drinking hours
don't recognise the laws of *perestroika*.
The black raven sharpens its beak.
The retired officers'
uniforms are scarlet.
They're all well-fed
and composed.
Our guide is a jaunty
ex-army lieutenant, a successful man.
He unfolds to us the history.
He speaks hurriedly above our heads
as though reading from the guide-book.
(Not in vain did Mars and Mercury align.)
He talks about Liz Stuart as though
she is a close relative.
His feet rest on the ground
like a medieval knight's.
He's a great chap,
a humanist and all.
But the Suez medal
is a stain on his uniform.
A chance visitor to this castle,
I converse with the centuries,

trailing their trains
over the paving-stones into tomorrow.
Blue Tower Bridge,
spans future and past,
and Hamlet's groans and his question
span fools and the intelligent.
In the dungeons I saw
various devices:
if you were particularly clever,
they would make you break in a trice.
But that's no surprise to us –
we know different tortures.
London, London, the chimneys on the roofs
take aim into the blue sky.
Yes, the spire sparkles like a brooch-pin,
yes, the military man is civil to the civilians.
There's room for hope
when there's dust on the cannon muzzles.
My trip was not in vain.
One can see the large in the small –
it's good that
the prison became a museum.

2

for Dima, postgraduate at Cambridge University

The mallows bloom in Cambridge.
Herds of Newtons rush around.
Comfort rules in Cambridge.
There is a smell of river and grass.
Every genius will be a Lord tomorrow,
and become a Nobel Laureate.
Meanwhile they're proud
of the atom's achievements.
The fourth son of the Duke of Kew,
who's going out with the porter's daughter,
swishes past on a bicycle.
The mallows are blooming in England.

The Lomonosovs
believe in something too,
and live comfortably.
Cambridge. On Silver Street
a young exchange post-graduate student
is talking to me about home,
and the smell of hay,
and that there is no medicine
for immune deficiency syndrome
of the conscience. He talks
directly of life here.
A country's brains and hands
cannot come into being without suffering.
The prince and the pauper are all equal
before science's Sisyphean mushroom.
If it had been like that with us,
ships would not have sunk,
bad people would not
have power at home,
grain would not rot,
joy would not be taken in battle,
foreign films would not
be cut by the censor.
AIDS of the soul is more terrible
than the white corpuscle in the red blood:
don't shove us into the cells of schemes,
homo homini is no match.
There are people – and there is the rabble.
(Origins are not relevant.)
If a worm has gnawed conscience,
then the soul cannot be saved.
We acquired the syndrome –
we have to suppress it.
Strolling with Dima
in Cambridge not long ago.
We walked down Silver Street,
two *glasnost* brothers,
and we talked about
how it wasn't bad to be alive.

VERONICA DOLINA

'If only our lives were trouble-free'

If only our lives were trouble-free,
I would give birth to children
fathered by all those who loved me,
children of every kind and hue.

As I stroked my fledglings' heads,
I would remember their fathers,
some of them family men,
others just youngsters.

They would lack for nothing,
family feuds would not touch them.
The fledglings of that nest
would be so unlike each other.

The wise man will teach the fool
how to live risk-free.
Let the fool teach the brother
that life is sweet to the taste.

The simplest sister will teach spinning,
the thief-sister will teach stealing.
The nun-sister will teach them
to pray that they go not astray.

When I grow old
I would gather
my dozen descendants
at the dinner table.

How unalike are the brothers,
but how happy to see each other!
This is the most important thing:
this is the bond.

If only our lives were trouble-free,
I would give birth to children
fathered by all those who loved me,
children of every kind and hue.

VLADIMIR DRUK

Aphasia

Are you still alive, O my infection?
   My corruption? My inflation?
Are you still alive, O my protection,
   My presumption? My infestation?
Are you still alive, O my tradition?
   My militia? My castration?
Are you still alive, my provinces?
   My education? My stagnation?
Are you still alive, O my formation?
   My construction? My abstraction?
Are you still alive, O my pollution?
   my prostration –

   I'm alive, I'll survive
   Happily ever after –
   What's it to you?

Only Just A Little Man

The poor thing's soul only just stays in his body.
In the mornings he can only just get up for work.
And in the evenings he can only just get home,
And he's only just living with his wife.

Their children only just managed to be born
And play quietly on the faded parquet.
Once he jumped through the window, head-first,
And the poor thing, he only just survived.

Television Centre

Stereopoem

'I spend my spare time in front of a television screen'

i am an ordinary natural scientist
i am certainly not a radio-ham
on my head there's a pick-up arm
and in my belly, a loudspeaker

but i've also got arms or legs
and i've also got a piston or a valve
to this day i've sat and never scratched myself
to this day i've sat and never made a squeak

policemen and teenagers
have stirred up the secret services
i just happened to be in the epicentre
the noise is stilled and i come out onto the stage[1]

the darkness of night is aimed at me[1]
and other photoelectric cells
ramakrishna, galich and korotich[2]
waited a long time for this moment

i want to tell such a tall story
i want to pull such a face
that those who never heard of such a thing
run off to report and denounce me

i want to find myself in such a phase
and then take such a dosage
that i'm instantly swept up into metastasis
without the narcosis of metamorphosis

a one
a one and a
two and a
laughter is my race-track
line frequency
frame frequency
frame purity
the party framework decides
                    everything
am i in the party framework?
requisitioning
the short circuit
with my own hands
Hail Caesar, Dosage!
stand up straight, hands on
shoulders out, arms raised
what d'you want, a golden fish?
i don't want to be
a crimean tartar
i just want to be
a tartar
No. 186 – 187
mon tue mon tue tue tue
7.00 sunrise °C
7.15 yesterday's news
7.47 it's still early
it's late!
ab
ovo
well here we are

i am an ordinary natural scientist
i am prepared for labour and defence
i can snap off a leafy birch-bough
and live on full board and lodgings

if you're not a member of nato
if you're on the register
we live in the same boarding-house
and we live by economic self-support

where people get sloshed despite the anti-drink
measures
where they sober up despite the wooden bunks
and hang around like crimean tartars
having got their permit to live in the Hotel
Angleterre[4]

where the rectifier doesn't rectify
but the transformer transforms
where you will become fully sober
if you disconnect the stabiliser

evri badi or evri bodi
hare krishna or hare rama
the cinerama rolls
for those who are at liberty

large-format formats
large-scale scales
highly-scientific sciences
deeply-wicked wickednesses

i run and run and run
i don't look after myself
to india
to america
on colour telly
B comes from A
C comes from B
therefore
C comes from A
you can't take one word
from a song without[3]
he looked at himself
for a long long time
without suspecting

that for ages he'd been
live on TV
1 am – 2 pm lunch

$1/6$ to the end of the world

i love you, Clink!
that speaks for itself of course

my running is powerful
broadchested
of course i could have had
some advantage from him
i blow the spittle from my lips

and puff smoke-rings
from my nostrils
Hail, Caesar!
what do you want, a golden fish
i don't want to be the agency

ineffective effects
ferro-concrete concretes
far-reaching ideas
multi-million millions

ooh yes costumes-and-props people
where are your creamy yoghourts?
where are your dressed-up homers?
where are your clandestine apartments?

he who lives as a hostage to events
also lives as a hostage to utopia
the tsarevich dmitri sleeps blissfully
he has slept through the european cup-final

i am an ordinary natural scientist
i am certainly not a radio-ham
if a common denominator is found
they'll find a common substitute

you are my electroquiz
you are my open terminal
sour like a snowball-tree berry
slender like a radio antenna

why are we like sardines in tomato-sauce?
and not like berries in a compote?
you are more high-principled in bed
than my supervisors at work

at this hour of nocturnal plasticine
i close the circuit of father and son
darling, let's make a cretin
a cheburashka[6] or a pinocchio

tass
i want to be the agency
mass
i don't want to be a doctor
hyde-r
i want to be ilya
glazunov
children of kisses
hairdressers of the world
left-liberal totalitarians
16.30 – military coup
direct transmission
17.47 – exact
time signals
hearing at the epicentre
fearing at the epicentre
co-ordinate axes
everyone has been called
and everything has been spoiled

9th March tuesday 17.30
and life
when you look at it
with cold attention[5]
is such a drying-out station!

here are thirty traffic-cops
blowing their whistles for attention
they run after me
from sheer boredom
and i trace their steps
john runs after me
and so does lennon
and thirty-two kilos

darling, let's make a blockhead
so he can emerge faster from the fog
so he can pull a knife from his pocket
and break the seal on the emergency-stop

...i am fit but heterozygotine
like an ordinary destroyer of nature
i can get sloshed in an aeroflot
or by drinking stain-remover

i love my air-base
with its managers who are so calm
where they heal my decay
where they teach me to think in prose

how much effort goes into ritual!
how much effort goes into procedures!
how many of them are scarabs and arabs?
how many of us are arabs and scarabs?

life is closed like a shop for the privileged
but open like an embrasure
the word 'death' is changed by the censor
a safety-device is concealed inside the rest

and then there's a thingummabob
and then there's a thingummajig
and then there's a johnnon or a lennon
and then there's a *mutter* or a *vater*

we will build a new accelerator
and achieve full disintegration
the last TV viewer will be wiped off
the documentary of the last parade

of cod
devil-dimwits
herbicide-pesticide
karabakh-tat-a-tat
go forward, fools!
go back, pinocchios!
stalingrad
stalingrad
stalingrad
no!
no!
no!
the third world war
will end with a world-wide
television
show
man is a ruby
man is a record
man is a horizon
our man
but now an electrolyte
pours into me
and the thrilling liquid
surges in me
this is me running
but perhaps it's him
who's running
on your TV
r.reagan – 493 points
f.mitterand – 607 points
m.canadians – 703 points
sorley – 917 points
23.15 – the second-to-latest news
23.55 – the latest news
00.00 hours
the end of the world

oh god! i am Your nomenklatura!⁷
oh god! i am Your nomenklatura!

00.07 hours – the end of the world

on video

1. *Quotations from Hamlet, by Pasternak ('Dr Zhivago', tr. Max Hayward and Manya Harari, Collins Harvill, 1987).*
2. *Alexander Galich was a ballad-singer, Vitaly Korotich is the editor-in-chief of the magazine, Ogonyok.*
3. *"You can't take one word from a song without changing it" – Russian proverb.*
4. *The Hotel Angleterre, Leningrad, was where Yesenin committed suicide.*
5. *A quotation from a famous poem by Mikhail Lermontov, "Iskuchna i Grustna".*
6. *Cheburashka – a cartoon animal on children's TV, naive, loveable and liable to misadventures.*
7. *Nomenklatura – the party elite.*

Genealogy

(from the cycle, 'Names')

A begat B
B begat C
C begat D
D begat D¹

Autoepitaph

(from the cycle, 'Names')

Here lies
vladimir druk,
poet-songwriter,
compère-joker,
doctor-orthodontist,

pedagogue-organiser,
artist-avantgardist,
chief-cook,
hero-lover,
universal-lathe-operator
humpty-dumpty,
actor-improviser,
flat-tenant,

horseman-maiden,
collective-farm-millionaire,
carrier-rocket,
Kamenets-Podolski,*
goodness-gracious,
scape-goat,
amateur-gardener,
nightingale-brigand,

yes, yes! it's me, it's me –
vladimir druk,
fruit-'n'-veg,
newspaper-novel,
hände-hoch[1],
major-general,
here i lie.

square-cluster-planted[2],
convexo-concave,
arithmetical-mean,
pugilistic-patriotic,
wines-'n'-spirits,
mamin-sibirak.**

Yes, yes! It's him, it's him –
vladimir druk,
crème-brûlée,
tête-à-tête,
full-speed-ahead,
phrasebook-dictionary,
here he lies.

no-room.
no-beer.
no-unauthorised-enclosures.
rest in peace, dear friend-druk![3]
        your alter ego...

*   *name of town*
**   *Russian writer, Dmitri Mamin Sibirak*
       (1852–1912)
1.   *hands up!*
2.   *agricultural term for sowing in squares*
3.   *'druk' is Russian for 'friend'*

MIKHAIL EISENBERG

'Oh, it was great!'

Oh, it was great! Such fun, such fun!
No it wasn't, it was terrible, terrible.

It was some sort of ghastly mess
of rumours, events, shit, good things,
tenderness and jealousy.
Nights were terrifying and out of fairy tales.
Light and claustrophobia.
The secret's out – we have drunk pure poison.
Good Lord, where are they ordering us to now,
that the sentence be carried out so sharply?
Sergeant major wallah, comrade with full powers to...

Even the hidden were herded,
and it was not always absurd.
There was something almost beautiful –
did we just live for nothing
counted only as slave labour?
Oh, for how many years had we got used
to the non-work discipline. What torture
to writhe back and forth in inherited convulsions!
Hot and cold. Desperately hot. Desperately alone.

Praises and glory to every one of you
who write with the remnants of language.
Glory to the starving writing paper
of all who, carried over the clouds,
have saved themselves from thirst by a miracle,
and die and sleep and are not,
and are not to be again.

SERGEI GANDLEVSKY

'Our country, betrayal, heroism'

To D. Prigov

Our country, betrayal, heroism...
Decades ago, an express train is racing along –
up ahead the track has been broken:
it seems a catastrophe is inevitable,
and there are people on board. The young pioneer
comes up and goes in to the emergency hut.
He takes off his red scarf
and waves the bright material.
The driver sees it from the engine
and realises that something is wrong.
He swiftly pulls the lever –
and the catastrophe is averted.

Or another example of how it used to be:
an express is racing along.
The track is broken up ahead.
It seems a catastrophe is inevitable,
and there are people on board.
The old pointsman goes in to the emergency hut,
slashes a vein with a store knife
and soaks a rag in the crimson, hot blood
and waves the bright material.
The driver sees it from the engine
and realises that something is wrong.
He swiftly pulls the lever –
and the catastrophe is averted.

But in our times, when trains run
the track is in good order as far as the eye can see.
Wonderful living conditions, study or work,
or combine work with a correspondence course.
Everything has changed. The young pioneer is no longer young.
He's grown a little flabby, and completely staid.
he's become a railway boss
and shouts at the old pointsman
and threatens to bury him in the modern wonders of transport.

'Oh, the lilacs this May!'

Oh, the lilacs this May! Burgeoning branches
lasso the villages and brush one's face
with their soulshattering perfume
in the darkness where the boulevards join.

Hold your heart in your hand, go as you will like a blindman.
Here a naked preschool boy met me on the boulevard,
a bowman with a crafty expression; look at him shoot that arrow!
Much water has flowed past since then. I think this too will pass.

Mornings I'd sit proudly with crossed legs by the entrance
to the chasm of the Metro with a spray of lilac in my arms.
I'd puff smoke rings from my nostrils and drink a lemonade in the rush hour.
I smiled and declared in my mind to my fellow citizens:

'Where are you rushing to, you fools? I'm nineteen, you idiots.
I've never had a job and I never will.
Do you know my secret? No you don't.
Last night I slept with Laisa. We cheated on Victor.'

POLINA IVANOVA

Windows

A window. It's so you can live
As if you were in the front row at the cinema.
It's so you won't sleep through till dawn.
A transparent thing. A window.

It's so you have something to break.
And if it's a moonlight night,
By the way, and you're forced to howl,
You won't find a better place.

It's so you can feel delirious,
Breathing in fumes, then heat.
It's so you can peer at a streetlamp,
A poplar tree, a pavement.

It's so you can see with dead certainty
How no-one is coming.
A window's for bringing the draught in
Till it hits the target – you.

It's so that you stop taking care of yourself,
Breathe frozen air, go mad.
It's so you can then be ill
For a long time. Feverish. Thrilled.

It's so you can kill a day,
And where, if it's night,
You can go away into yourself.
And where all the rest of the nonsense

– For which 'thank you' and 'very much' –
Can be dumped like a load from your shoulder.
A window is so you can try, and be unable.
Spit through it, and lie down.

And it's for your evil epilogue.
You're alive, you're by the iron bars.
You press your face to them.
You push your face through, among leaves,
And your face grows leaf-like.

It's so you can feel something's not right
Till you're under the planks of your coffin,
And passing away from your love
And passing away from your yearning.

'No-one's here'

No-one's here. This is twilight. Raindrops and twilight.
No-one's here. These are raindrops and twilight. Links invisible.
A blurred country scene. A pantomime of shadows
Fluttering in like butterflies towards lamp-light.

But still no-one's here. Raindrops and twilight. There
The long wings are folded, quiver like dragonflies.
No-one's here. These are shadows, declaring war on the body.
Their bonds weaken, they slowly change position.

But still no-one's here. These are the outlines of outlines.
They find themselves by filling space with themselves.
The darkness finds that its destiny is to be
A crush of curved lines. These are raindrops and twilight. Horrible.

The darkness comes to life. It is burning matter.
It gives birth to movement and movement is born. And it cuts.
Darkness cuts matter. All is soothed and pleased.
And electricity tells lies in the darkness

Because no-one is in it. Electricity lies. There's no-one.
These are raindrops and twilight. Raindrops and twilight. The theme.
Invisible to us, the soul is not leaving
The solitary totem, his solitary form.

TIMUR KIBIROV

When Lenin was Little

(Extracts)

I

Ilya Nikolayevich, Vladimir Ilyich's father, was at that time an inspector of schools in the Simbirsk province. He was from simple origins and had lost his father at an early age and his elder brother had helped him to get his education, which was not easy...

Maria Alexandrovna, Vladimir Ilyich's mother, was the daughter of a doctor; she spent most of her early life in the village, where the peasants loved her. She was a good musician – she had a good knowledge of music and knew French, German and English...

A.I. Ulyanova 'Childhood and school years of Ilyich' Detgiz, 1947, p.4.

I often think of how... It's true, it's strange
to imagine it. But it really did happen!
Otherwise he could not have been born.
And so, although the mind cannot take it in,
to bring about his appearance on earth,
for his writing of 'What is to be Done?'
and the 'Three Sources of Marxism', and 'Aurora',
for the plan of the State Electricity, for the moon walk,
for the atom walk – for everything! –
the spermatozoid (just one!) had to pierce
into the childbearing organ of Maria Alexandrovna...
How strange...

I imagine their little house in Simbirsk.
The year is 1869. The twilight is blue.
The inspector is in the study. The comforting light
of the table lamp lights his Socratic
forehead. Pen scratches on paper...
Suddenly and quietly a melody
sounds from the distant rooms –
with such measureless tenderness,
such a heavenly, eternal, feminine sadness...
A sweet dreaminess grasped
his active brain. His hand froze,
and he stopped writing... He put out the light,
got up and walked out on tiptoe.

In the drawing room Maria Alexandrovna was sitting
at the grand-piano without the light on.
Ilya lingered by the door, involuntarily
admiring the slender, sad, silhouette
of his wife against the background of the window.
Time flew, and the melody grew in deep sadness
and unspoken love and the promise of happiness, and tears...
Finally he coughed. 'Oh, darling,
you gave me a fright!' – 'Maria!' the inspector's voice
was hoarse and deep with tenderness: 'It's late,
time to go to bed, Maria!' and there was something in his voice
that made Maria Alexandrovna blush.
'Oh, darling, what do you...' – 'Mashenka, let's go up!
Let's go, it's late, come on little Masha!...'

I think she was frigid;
or almost frigid and reluctantly shared
the inspector's passion,
not immediately, but then entwining
the powerful torso of the inspector of schools
with tender hands and tender legs:
Ilya, Ilyushechka, Ilyushechka... Darling Ilyusha!

IV

*Young Vladimir loved to catch birds and set traps for them with
his mates. I remember he had a linnet in a cage. I don't know if
he had caught it, bought it or been given it. But I do remember
that it didn't live long, sulked, pined away and died. I do not
know why this happened, or whether Volodya was to blame for
not feeding the bird. I only remember that someone chided him
about this and I remember the serious concentration with which
he looked at the dead linnet, and his saying decisively: 'I won't
keep birds in cages any more.' He kept his word.*

A.I. Ulyanova 'Childhood and school years of Ilyich' Detgiz,
1947, p.18.

Little linnet, fly in the swarm of shadows,
to where the blind swallow has returned,
where the doves of Cypros circle,
where Lesbia's sparrow is, where the wounded
Falcon greets the flight of its friend the Stormy Petrel,
where the terrifying albatross that's been killed
avenges sternly the English sailor, where the French sailors
won back a similar revenge on another similar albatross,
where the country man shoots down the seagull,
where the nightingale is over the rose, where the bullfinch
sings a martial song, where even the lapwing
sings to the young naturalists by the side of the road,
where the starling is on the branch, where raven
either flies to raven or to crazy Edgar
in the midnight hour, where songs flow
between sky and Russian earth,
where chickens want to live, where you can hear
the tiny little voice of the robin,
where the singer, according to an ancient custom,
set free a bird without a name,
where the hen is speckled, where the Kingfisher
darts over Batyushkov's sail, where Philomel
whistles and murmurs in the dark night,

where the bird of happiness will choose you,
where the Eaglet flew above the sun,
where the blind swallow, the blind...
Little linnet, fly there,
fly there: you deserve your immortality!

V

He used to go fishing in the Sviyaga river in Simbirsk. One of his mates tells the story of how one of the kids suggested they try catching fish in a big ditch filled with water nearby, saying that there were good carp there. They went to it, but Volodya leaned over and fell in; the muddy bottom was sucking him down. 'I don't know what would have happened,' his friend said, 'if a worker from the factory on the river bank had not heard our cries, and come running and dragged Volodya out.'

A.I. Ulyanova 'Childhood and school years of Ilyich' Detgiz, 1947, p.19.

The Worker's hand saved the Fatherland.
Whatever the Social Democrats say,
everything would have turned out differently
without this person's role. Mother Russia
was all ready to glide down Bourgeois rails –
and would indeed have done so –
down the sloping surface, so to speak,
down the vicious track
of least resistance. No doubt it would have
searched out the easiest ways for itself,
and it would have decayed. How it would have decayed!
To this day they would have eaten pineapple
and had grouse for dinner; and I very much doubt
whether the Belomor canal would have been dug.

They wouldn't have overcome prostitution!
And the Bloody Tsar Nicholas would have lived,
unpunished, with his wife and children.
Intelligence, honour, conscience would have continued
to languish in Shushensky. And our Serafimovich
would have been exposed to the mockery
of cynical, corrupt modernists. And, by God,
Yevtushenko would have had to perform
in taverns in Odessa... It's terrible to think about.
But there is another thing that's terrible to think about
but interesting – how about if not a *worker*
but a peasant called Marey or Platon,
had dragged him out of the mud?
What if our Ilyich had fallen for
the humble wisdom and sense of mission of the ordinary people?
Would he have adopted the simple life
and travelled through Russia like a beggar, blessing it the while?
Oh, how strange. Or imagine a fine merchant
had been passing? Or a tall guardsman?
Or a priest's son in a college jacket:
that is one of those from the pack of hounds and executioners?
And would our little Volodya have become a cadet?
And there would have been no spring blossoming
and call to victory... Oh, how strange it is,
how strange it all is, if one thinks about it a little.

1985

OLEG KLEBNIKOV

'An old woman'

'We're not reddish-golden fish' – Osip Mandelstam

An old woman – the most dangerous neighbour
On public transport.
She carries her lunch in her bag
– Herring, bread and onion.

The herring marinade drips out.
The onions are grimy.
No-one wants to give her their place
– Not the small fry and not the big fish.

So she aims her bony elbow
Straight into your ribs.
Her lifeless mouth gasps half air
And half despair.

Anyway, we're not dumb, we're not fish.
It's our custom to complain
And not be afraid of a mouth
Open before its death.

Five heels to an inch. Humidity
Like that which brews thunder.
But where the old woman stands,
It's still possible to breathe.

1989

VLADIMIR KOSTROV

'What use are passport formalities?'

What use are passport formalities?
We won't get out anyway.
Here we shall sin and confess,
rise and perish,
and eat burnt Russian porridge
with pepper and blood.
Disaster is our constant metaphor –
never ending, never got rid of.
We must love Nadson and Hikmet
rather than Gogol.
In the state farms, under The New Economic Plan,
on the heights, and in the depths,
on earth and in heaven,
in forgiveness and sin.
What use are passport formalities.
We can't get away from ourselves!

VICTOR KOVAL

Monologue of the Expert

(sung by Andrei Lipski)

In evaluating creatively
squandered banknotes,
I, the expert, cannot keep quiet
about my love for the cherished
seven-coloured impressions
and the lofty Orlov imprints.
I sniff the engravings,
etched with gold,
the reddish one-rouble note
whose carbolic money smell
wafts like the scent
of a brown leaf in autumn,
breathing off rotting
brownish ochre.
Rustling, shouting,
crisping, of Ugro-Mongolian origin,
banknotes, smelling sweet as women,
my seven-toned engravings,
not fancy sweet wrappings,
integral as the original units of currency.

In November, in October
in February and in the Tsars' times
the single rouble note in its warm tones:
See and believe – it's all in the colour.

Sometimes I get up
and go to the window
and look out at the view
and remember the three rouble note.

The palace garden is green
by the Water tower,
and Fearless Ivan
is standing over the letter 'L'.
Ah money, money, big money,
means, fines, phenomenal money..
towers, heads, green standards,
seven-toned engravings,
not fancy sweet wrappings,
triple roubles — real money.

In November, in October
in February and in the Tsars' times
the three rouble note in its green tones:
See and believe – in the cold tones.

And in the cold wind
when I stand for hours
at the place of execution
I look at St Saviour's tower
and beyond a pale blue Christmas tree
under a dark blue star
a blue five rouble note
is lying in front of me.
Ah money, money, big money,
means, fines, phenomenal money..
Ah titti-mitti, fivery fivers,
Seven-toned fivers are not fancy sweet wrappers:
fivesome five sums, blue-black brigands.

In November, in October
in February and in the Tsars' times
the five rouble note in its blue tones:
See and believe – in blue-black tones.

But the dark red 'State ticket'
is crimson as the dawn
and the simple portrait
warms the hand so pleasantly
gazing expansively
framed by the Rococo east.

In November, in October
in February and in the Tsars' times
the ten rouble note in its red tones:
See and believe – in its hot tones.

Ah money, money, big money,
means, fines, phenomenal money..
Money, ancient money, rouble, some sums of sums,
seven-toned engravings,
They're not fancy sweet wrappers
but the caramels themselves that come from Karakum.

The Silver Hake

(sung by Andrei Lipski)

I'll not wait for my silver
hake fish supper
but leave the house
without saying goodbye to my wife.
I'll see as I go out
the wooden lime tree
the watery stream
Vera Veremeyevna

I see the Christmas fir tree
the atmospheric sky
and Vera Veremeyevna
out of sorts again.
Oh flat plain,
seen from everywhere,
I shouted 'Gentlemen,
where the hell are you?
The years that have been lived are gone,
the years of good living have come.
Where were you, where on earth are you,
and how are you?'

I returned home to the wife
and she shouted at me:
'You home-wrecker, oh Lord
where is the devil leading you to
for God's sake.
Look the truth in the eye:
our days are all lived out,
where were you, my only one,
how could you, how could you?

I've no intention of
tormenting myself by staying with you.
Let Veremeyevna, the marriage-breaker
feed you.
Look, your frozen hake
has got cold on the plate.
My God, my Lord, you've driven me
round the bend,
worse than hake with horse radish
worse than treacle hake
than silver hake
hake hake
hic haec hoc hake'

VICTOR KRIVULIN

'It is Difficult'

It is difficult for the visionaries at the meeting
in the orifice of the hungry mouth
A line of men draws up alongside
the confused militia man
There aren't enough roofs for me
under the skies of my native land,
there is not enough old-testament power
in the clouds nor enough air and water for all.
We complain to each other
but it's not clear what we're on about.
Our body is bound tight then unswaddled
as though it has no arms and it stretches its tired limbs
and squints at the weak sun and is blinded
after the warm inner-womb universe
where there was darkness and blood

'Deserted, but thirsting'

Deserted but thirsting to fill themselves,
with that swollen ancient feeling of giving birth,
they are drawn to the East to the rising smoke
to the burnt villages

if the flames are going to engulf us too,
there is a hidden reason for this:
the fire was a common one and raced through the air,
and this fire changed its masks –

it was salty, earthy drilled
into the brain forcibly and from outside,
this is how an overturned stall is set alight,
full of burned out truth

VYACHESLAV KUPRIANOV

Thirst

Childhood
Is a well of timelessness

Youth,
A well of expectation

Old age,
A sip of water.

Twilight Vanity

Every night
A dead man
Lifts the slab of his tomb
And tests with his fingertips

Whether anyone has scraped
The name from the stone.

A 24-Hour Grammar

The weighty nouns of daytime:
Service
Concern
Hope

The frail adverbs of evening:
Quietly
Tremulously
Wearily

The reflexive verbs of night:
To be met with
To part from
To forget oneself

The bright prepositions of morning:
To the stars
From the heart
In the beginning

Anticipation

Darling,
Wait a minute.
Don't go.
Give me one more day
To find out the secret
Of how we live
So that these days of ours
Stay ours for always.

Children,
Wait a minute.
Don't grow up so fast.
Give me one more year
To find out the secret
Of how to live by your side,
Sharing these years of yours
Without repeating
My mistakes.

Mother,
Wait a minute.
Don't get old.
Give me one more life-time
So I can return
At least a fragment
Of all you've given me.

Life,
Wait a minute...

TATIANA KUZOVLEVA

The Woman and Perestroika

Days are replaced by more days.
Year swiftly follows year.
The woman with the heavy bags
Walks the length of the USSR.

She wears grey or green or crimson...
What does it matter? The sight
Of her hooped shoulders must surely
Cut you men to the heart?

And the way she wearily trudges
The eternally dug-up street,
And wheezingly sighs: you get soaked
With sweat as you drag home the lot.

What's she got – seven-times-seven
Baby jackdaws that want to be fed,
Or a hoard of ravenous offspring
That came from a giant's seed?

On the contrary. It's more usual
In the Soviet Union
For our families to have two children.
Then why are all these bags
Attached to this miserable woman?

Supposing she threw them away?
'Sod them!' Woman, who cares
About sausages? We lose
Our identity in the names
People shout at us on the street.

And in queuing and rushing we've lost
The habit of smiling. Men,
In your intellectual circles,
Aren't you conscience-stricken?

Look hard. The wounded ones
With eyelashes lightly trembling
And faces worn away
By the carrying of bags
– These are the women you love.

You often make quite a picture
As you hotly debate the issues:
Multi- or one-party system?
Private farm or collective?

Don't waste any more time devising
Your schemes. It's seventy years
Since October. The woman still walks
With her heavy shopping-bags.

YUSUS MATZAVICHUS

Conclusion

It is not time that urges on the clock hands,
and not fairies that perform miracles.
Lips grow old by themselves,
arteries to the heart get clogged.

Time calculates you on its fingers,
like a savage or a philosopher,
who does not know that the seed
grows to die in the ripened ear.

YUNNA MORITZ

'The next two generations'

The next two generations will change their minds
As they leaf through the pages of our tragedy,
And shuddering, give much harsher names than we did
To the chemistry of events, their property and composition.

We should tear everything out, including the guts,
So as to see all these ulcers, all these scars
And all this pain that bleeds poems
Wherever our vagrants and lost people live.

It won't be the womanizers of 30 or 40,
Withered and searching, who'll make the discoveries,
But the children and teenagers who roam the parks
– Because their loneliness is full of insight.

And, recalling our own hopeful tremors, they will smile
Sadly at us as we leave,
As if benevolent smiles could swaddle the babies
Cut down by Herod early in the morning

– Yet not cut down... Today is Sunday
And in the silvery water there are branches
Of pussy-willow. This plant may be the place
In which hope can begin to glimmer as nowhere else.

'Poetry is being alive'

From *The Bitterness of Former Tortures*

Poetry is being alive, lovingly, freely;
Being alive is hard labour, prison, exile
And the slaughter-house where people are counted as cattle,
And the few are swallowed by the majority.

But shelters are everywhere, secret places, asylum:
There's a crack in the wall, a light in the stranger's window.
Poems hide themselves in a snowdrift, a boot or a mouth,
In the mind or the wash-tub, haystack or rotting tree-stump.

Wretched Adam, ex-military instructor,
Is questioned by his young grandson: "Where were you
When Ruslan[1] guarded Mandelstam's broken mind?"
"I was with the majority. He was with the few."

Poems are hidden by the minority will
In pipes and geometry-sets, on the devil's horns,
So when there's a rumour that poetry's still alive
Or sudden news of a great minority, torn

And devoured by that blood-bespattered humanophobe
With his small-pox scars and moustache, that Lilliput
With his pack of slaves waiting to lick his coffin,
The majority has a clear conscience after all.

Poetry's soul doesn't shrink from misfortune.
The freedom of poetry won't be stopped by the dead
Nor the living. Poets are few, but they let us breathe,
They give us breath after breath
– Even through a straw, to the sea-bed.

1. *Ruslan – the prison-camp guard-dog in Georgy Vladimov's famous novel, 'Faithful Ruslan'.*

OLESIA NIKOLAYEVA

Seven Beginnings

1

Coming out of the city
    Where new buildings, new occupants and upstarts
        Are in control,
Wishing to become somebody, wishing to be happy,
    Reassuring yourself that hell is not so terrible,
Oh boldest of women, my soul,
    Don't lift your proud head any higher,
Don't look back!

2

Coming out of the city
    Where someone loved so-and-so,
Where someone was playing Mozart's best sonata
    For somebody else
And the grand piano was totally out of tune,
    Where Eros's nose was peeling
        And the gilt fell like dust from Orpheus,
Oh don't look back.

3

Coming out of the city
    Where birthdays were being celebrated
        And people gave weight to fashionable opinions,
Where people said when they met at the funeral party
    "Just fancy, we've not seen each other for ages"
        And drank wine and plucked grapes
When they were sick with melancholy and cancer,
    Where they murdered children in the womb
        And assisted at the birth,
Oh don't look back.

4

Coming out of the city
    Where clothes, shoes and a full table
    Were over-rated,
Where people were asking themselves,
    "Why is this necessary? What am I getting out of it?"
Where they tried to prove that goodness
    Ought to use its fists,
Oh don't look back, my soul, but look ahead.

5

Coming out of the city
    That was looked back on by the just man's wife
Because not every love turned cold
    And memories tear the breast
And not every arrow vanishes
    And not every string bends,
But oh my soul, oh my soul,
    Forget all about this.

6

Coming out of the city
    Where one cupola is still golden
And one bell in the high tower
    Assures you of this:
That every word is dead,
    And not one tear will return to its origins,
Oh my soul, don't look back
    Or you will be as still as a pillar of salt.

Olesia Nikolayeva

7

Coming out of the city
    That's already defeated, lying in its ashes,
Where there's no-one to mourn their dead
Oh don't look back, my soul,
    Forget, be deaf, be blind
When God leads you out of your father's city.

DENIS NOVIKOV

'Homesick for familiar places'

Homesick for familiar places,
in a deep and innocent sleep,
the MI-22, all Russian bird,
scans the waste land.

A shadow on the sand troubles it,
he squeezes the cannon trigger with his iron hand
and spies a rowan branch
floating down the Oka river.

A rush of nostalgia,
wide open and on the outside,
soaring with its broad soul
he notices the soul alongside

of that shaky shadow on the sand
which without knife or revolver
flies, like a ball on a string
in the hand of an unshaven gipsy...

Back home his elder sister
wiped and set the right number of plates,
and put the branches in the jaws of the bonfire
and the strings on the guitar.

Ponies and sledges. Clear ice.
The rod bending from the fish.
The helicopter salivates
and trembles like a curtain,

and makes for home,
guided by an internal signal
and continues to sleep sweetly
through the whole military tribunal.

BULAT OKHUDZHAVA

From *Dedicated to You*

'A poet has no rivals in fate'

A poet has no rivals in fate
And none in his every-day life.
Each time he declaims to the world
It's not about you, but himself.

He lifts his thin arms to the sky.
He sweats out his strength, burns dim
As a candle, and asks forgiveness
– Not for you but for him.

When he reaches the end of his time
And his soul flies into the shadows,
When the field has been crossed, the deed done,
You must decide what his life was.

Whether bitter or sweet, whether holy
Or ravaged by war, ripped in two,
Whatever was his, is now yours.
All yours. Dedicated to you.

1988

'I was going to visit my mother'

I was going to visit my mother – she was dead.
I wanted to see my father. He had been shot.
The shadow of the black eagle from Gori
        covered all the world.

Shadow-stained, sickened by yells of triumph,
I want to ask that wretched lot a question
While they're still as wretched as ever.

I was going to visit my mother – she was dead.
I wanted to see my father. He had been shot...
        Why did you forget to ask me
        As you did your magnificent deeds
        If I needed my mother and father?
        What was your philosophy all about?

DMITRI PRIGOV

Kulikovo[1]

So I set them all in their places
Put these on the right
Put those on the left
Kept all the others till later
I kept the Poles till later
I kept the French till later
And I kept the Germans till later
I put my angels in their places
I put the crows above them
And I put the other birds high up
But I saved the field below
I saved it to be a battlefield
I covered it with trees
I covered it with oaks and spruces
I dotted some parts with bushes
I spread it with soft grass
I populated it with small insects
Let everything be as I imagined
Let everyone live as I willed it
Let everyone die as I willed it

So today the Russians will win
They're not bad boys, the Russians
And Russian girls aren't bad
They've suffered a lot, the Russians
Suffered many non-Russian horrors
So today the Russians will win

What will the future be like
If the earth has already crumbled
And the sky is already dusty
And the underground rocks collapse
And the underground waters rage
And the underground creatures rage
And the surface people run about
The earthbound run here and there
And the birds soar above the earth
And all the birds above the earth are crows?

Still, the Tartars are nicer
Yes, their voices are nicer
And their names are nicer
And their habits are nicer
Though the Russians are tidier
Still, the Tartars are nicer

So let the Tartars win
And then I'll be able to see everything
OK, let the Tartars win
Anyway, tomorrow it will all be clear.

1. *Kulikovo – the famous battle in 1380 in which the Russians
   for the first time defeated the Mongolian Tartars.*

'The plumber goes out into the wintry yard'

The plumber goes out into the wintry yard.
He looks round, and it's spring already.
This is exactly his own position.
He was once a schoolboy. Now he's a plumber.

And there's more to come. There's death,
And before death, senility,
And before that, and before that, and before
That, there's what he is: a plumber.

'Here I am, frying a chicken'

Here I am, frying a chicken –
It's sinful to make a fuss,
So I don't. But what can it mean
– That I'm better than everyone else?

I can't go on, I'm ashamed.
"Well I'm damned!" is all I can say
– To think that the nation has ruined
A whole chicken – just for me.

'In the Ready-to-Cook Department'

In the ready-to-cook department
I purchased a kilo of fish salad.
So what? It's no disgrace.
I simply made a purchase.
I ate a tiny bit
And I fed some to my own son.
We sat down by the window,
Beside the transparent glass
Like two male pussy-cats,
Letting life pass by below.

'Our Lord skims through the book of life'

Our Lord skims through the book of life:
"Who shall I get rid of?" he thinks.
A metallic noise in the sky is just audible
And people dash home like mice.

Smiling, he lifts up a roof,
Gropes around in the corners
And catches a poor man who shivers
And struggles, "Why" he asks softly,
"Do you struggle? God is with you."

'From one side'

From one side, the people are understandable.
From the other, they're inexplicable.
It all depends which side you're on,
Whether you find them understandable or inexplicable.

But you are understandable to them
From any side. And from any side inexplicable.
You're surrounded, you have no sides
So you can't be understood – or otherwise.

LEV RUBENSHTEIN

Mummy Washed the Floor

1   Mummy washed the floor.
2   Daddy bought a TV.
3   It was windy.
4   Zoya was stung by a wasp.
5   Sasha Smirnov broke his leg.
6   Borya Nikitin cracked his head on a rock.
7   It was raining.
8   One brother was teasing the other.
9   The milk boiled over.
10   The first word was the word "knee".
11   Yura Stepanov rigged up a hut.
12   Yuliya Mikhailovna was strict.
13   Vova Avdeev used to fight.
14   Tanya Chirikova is a fathead.
15   Galya Fomina's fellow only has one arm.
16   Sergei Alexandrovich had a telephone installed.
17   The invalid burnt to death in the car.
18   We were walking to the woods.
19   Grandma had cancer.
20   Grandma died in her sleep.
21   I often dream of grandma.
22   I was really scared of dying in my sleep.
23   Igor Dudkin looked like a Georgian.
24   Sergei Alexandrovich was joking with daddy.
25   The Sorokins had plums, but they had Blackie too.
26   The lads were playing volleyball in the clearing.
27   Gleb Vyshinskii brought a mouse.
28   Volodya Voloshenko told lies.
29   Elena Illarionova knew Sasha Chernii.
30   At the same time the tension was reduced.
31   There was an interesting film at the cinema.
32   My brother was winding up the record-player.
33   Daddy was bawling.
34   The brawler was clanking his chain.

35   Sasha Smirnov envied my stamps.
36   He could wiggle his ears.
37   Then I learned how to do it too.
38   Polina Mironova said her little Boris was an idiot.
39   Klavdiya Efimova's husband was called Mikhail Borisovich.
40   Raisa Savel'evna worked as an accountant in
      Food Store No. 40.
41   Yurii Vinnikov was her son.
42   Kseniya Alekseevna was a totally simple but very good woman.
43   Pavlik and Rita Aronov lived in the next block of flats.
44   By the way, Tanya Chirikova also lived in that block.
45   Unfortunately I can't remember the name of Raika Guseva's
      husband.
46   It was windy.
47   My brother told me what mummy and daddy were doing in the next
      room.
48   Sorrel, radish and leek also grew.
49   Slava Novozhilov had a scar from a wire club.
50   It was raining.
51   I was scared of Tanya Beletskaya's doll.
52   Yura Stepanov's father had no teeth, his mother was fat and his
      sister was a thickhead.
53   The sister's name was Yulya.
54   I didn't have a sister but I had a brother.
55   My brother said, Stalin died today.
56   My brother hit me because I laughed and pulled faces.
57   Daddy gave up smoking.
58   We hoped there would be war as soon as possible.
59   We loved the Chinese.
60   I wasn't allowed to cross the road.
61   Once I was almost suffocated by fumes.
62   Galya Fomina studied at teacher training college. When I
      asked her why it rained, she started to explain,
      beginning with:
      "In our country there are many lakes and rivers..."
              The rest I didn't understand and have forgotten.
63   Sasha Smirnov was in the habit of farting indoors.
64   You couldn't hear it but it really stank.
65   He wouldn't admit that it was him.

66   I learnt to ride a bike.

67   I was embarrassed at telling people my name.

68   Once I saw such an enormous caterpillar that even now I
      can't forget it.

69   I felt sick and vomited.

70   Once, entering Galya Fomina's room without knocking, I saw
      for the first time.

71   However, seized by a terrible premonition, I rushed out.

72   They came but much later than expected.

73   The wind raged all night and there was a thunderstorm too.

74   The weather was awful, everything was altered and dripping.

75   The wind blew from round the corner, it brought cold and
      misery.

76   Thunder roared, anguish and confusion seethed in one's breast.

77   The darkness whistled and flashed, hail clattered dreadfully on the
      roof.

78   The tips of the fir trees quivered, heavy clouds hung above the
      porch.

79   In the beginning it was like a beginning but in the end everything
      ended.

80   Everything overhead was the same as before, but underfoot the
      ground trembled.

81   They whirled and fell and swam and went off in all directions.

82   That day everything was the same as usual.

83   I got up, got dressed.

GENNADY RUSAKOV

In Transit

We really are a sad country –
the distances are to blame.
Funerals and weddings, drunken tears,
hangovers, heaviness, boring confessions.

A dry snowflake flutters on my fate.
Ricks, forests, jackdaws and crows.
8,000 miles of uncoordinated peasant dances.
Platforms trampled to death.

Samovars with wild, boiling water.
Bunks, buffets, frozen water-towers.
(Why and for whom am I saying this?)
And cigarettes from a sodden packet.

A crooked shadow leapt to the canvas.
I don't remember if it was twilight or dawn.
I will wail, I will call, I will curse!
Rubbish – we haven't the strength to scream.

Such a lonely, isolated country,
such a low sky, such a tormented soul.
Bitter station names.
Blackthorn, Mud... Pass on.

1989

VLADIMIR SAVELIEV

'It was not below the mighty hammer and sickle'

It was not below the mighty hammer and sickle
but on a woodland path that I met Molotov,
no longer under guard, no longer great.
In shabby trousers and jacket, crumpled cap,
everything about him down-at-heel,
he was just an ordinary old man from Zhukovka.[1]

Still I had to shake off the sinister apprehension
that he was the chief of vast organisations
– Narkomindel[2] and even Sovnarkom[3].
Those closest to him he did not consider close.
He could send people straight to the firing-squad,
one by one, or whole lists of them.

He cut down the forest with his henchmen.
He cut it down, and the trunks flew like splinters
on every side and sky-high. Near Barvikha[1],
in the part of the forest that remained unfelled,
I stared into the quiet face. Molotov
himself. Just think. The man himself.

A grandad wearing pince-nez.
But his portraits were certainly hung all over our cities
and in the wild Russian heartland,
as signs of his distinction under Stalin.
Our narrow path diverged, led windingly
into different epochs. To the death.To eternity.

1. *Areas near Moscow where many of the nomenclatura have their dachas*
2. *The People's Commissariat of Foreign Affairs*
3. *The Soviet of People's Commissars*

OLGA SEDAKOVA

A Chinese Journey

(extracts)

Azarovka, August 1986

8

The roofs are raised at the edges
like eyebrows in surprise.
What do you mean? Really? I'm happy to the bottom of my heart
From these terraces everything
dear to man
can be seen eternally:
the dry banks,
the silver-yellow rivers,
the scrawled letter of the bushes –
a love note –
Two passers-by bow
low to each other on the pontoon bridge
and a swallow brings the height
in on a tea
spoon.
Heart drops,
healing potion.
However, no one is sick in China,
for the sky itself is an expert
at acupuncture.

9

Unhappy
is the person who thinks of tomorrow while talking with his guest
Unhappy
is the person who does something and thinks that *he* does it,
and not that the air and sunlight rule it,
like a brush,
a butterfly
a bee,
he who plays a chord and thinks
of what comes next.
Even more unhappy
is the person who does not forgive:
he doesn't know that the stork comes out tame from the bushes,
that the golden ball
will soar of its own accord
into the dear sky over the dear earth.

10

Great
is the artist
who knows no debt
except for his debt to the brush's play
and his brush
enters into
the heart of mountains
enters into
the happiness of leaves
with one stroke
with one gentleness
rapture
confusion
with one gesture he enters into immortality
and immortality
plays

with him.
But he whom
the spirit
has deserted,
from whom the light
has been taken,
who, for the tenth time
in a muddy place
searches for the pure spring,
which fell from the hand of miracles
but will not say: 'These miracles are false!':
before
this person
the skies bow
submissively.

EKATERINA SHEVELYOVA

Hoping for Magic

Perhaps long before the baptism of Russia
The hearts of those distant people began to glimmer
And they prayed to the unknown at the tops of their voices:
"Save us!"

    – Hoping for magic.

Centuries passed. Then came accursed Judas
Who sold Christ, and the greatest suffering
Fell upon the greatest of all people
    With their hope of magic.

Folk-tales spoke of a hidden precious metal
And free-flying dreams brought golden fantasies;
Johnny-Hunchback soared into the city
    In the hope of magic.

Time and again the hero met his match.
Time and again he took his stand against
Devilish dreams, guarding the fields and forests,
    Hoping for magic.

For what reason was mankind allowed
This haughty insignificance, on loan?
Let it be damned for the rest of time
    – The hope of magic!

Now the doctor is mumbling:
"That's the way it is"
And I drag the hope with which every century burns
From its hiding-place, unthinkingly once more
    Hoping for magic.
Hoping for magic.

Memo about 1968

(Extracts)

2

August 21st.
                    Dawn is breaking.
I am on duty at the Novosti News Agency
– Not one other colleague in the dim-lit hall.
The teleprinters are silent.
                              A single one issues half-nonsense
In exchange for half-truths:
A rich man left millions to a dog,
A cataclysm has been forecast
                    by astrologers.
Suddenly
          the whole hall was in a flutter like a startled bee-hive.
The teleprinters rushed off as if from a starting-block:
'Soviet troops are entering Prague!'
The tapes grew like snow-heaps
(Suggested a forest clothed in white)
But in me there was only this silent prayer
For the young shoot, like a stubborn boy,
That my strange vision foresaw,
Breaking and entering life
                    in opposition to the party of dogmatists,
To survive its fragile conception
Under the metal bootsole
                    in the shattered night.

4

I judge myself far more severely now
Than at the time of the catastrophe.
I was like a blind beggar-woman
In those days, or so it seems to me
– A beggar-woman with some odds and ends
Of information, altered more than once,
Together with a feeble understanding
Of Czechoslovakia – all it means to us.

I gaze into the past intently, through
The troubles of our present great campaign
And the meeting I recorded on the page
Of my notebook, is before my eyes again...

... Western Czechia.
     The cry began
With winging catchwords, rose from all sides:
"Don't give them any food,
Don't give a drop of drink to Brezhnev's men!"

Spat at, caked with dust, they came;
They were undrilled in politics.
Sub-machine-gunners was their name,
Their appearance, that of boys.
Someone had commanded them
Not to react to jeers and spits.

They marched straight-backed and disciplined,
But thirst tormented them,
And now they were almost level with the buildings
Of the Imperial Convalescent Home.

Doctor Kveta told me:
        "All I did
Was give them tea. The managers and nurses
Swore at me and threatened
"You'll be black-listed". They had hidden
Everything, even the stale crusts.

"It was simply tea I gave them.
And I gave it to them not as soldiers
But as young lads, perhaps the sons of those
We glorified in Prague in '45
For having saved, simply, our people's lives."

This slender, clear-eyed Czech, a young mother
And clever doctor, couldn't comprehend
Why all these fellows had been got together
And sent to Prague, and called a regiment.

5

Carlovy Vary.
        Spa the world knows about.
Healing water. Picturesque mountains.
In Carlovy Vary that much-mentioned year,
The liveliest place of all was a tennis-court
Where, alongside the games, were conversations
About this and that.
        Someone let slip a phrase
(In which you can detect the hidden meaning)
That the freedom-loving European mind
Wants to preserve the beauty of such places.

When, on court or elsewhere, play grew excited,
We followed the battle with close attention.
And once, a journalist-pal from Washington
Sat down beside me on the bench. (United
By the free-thinking atmosphere around us,
We often had a friendly altercation.)
He said:
            "By the way, it wasn't sporting,
To send the Soviet troops in.

"Czechoslovakia, geographically
At least, is close to Moscow at first sight.
But Czech dreams are different. Gladness, sadness
Are different here. *'Mentalita'**, they call it."
He turned to his neighbour. "I'm right,
Don't you agree?" The man remained silent.
Then he glanced towards the mountainside.
"I don't know. Ask that path.
A weight of legends lies there, centuries-thick,
And not just legends, maybe true stories.
According to these stories, Poles and Czechs
And Russians lived on this same mountainside..."

* *Mentalita – Czech word for mentality*

ELENA SHVARTS

Orpheus

On the return
He took fright –
There was a wheezing and whistling behind him,
A grunting and coughing.

Eurydice:– Don't dare to glance aside,
          This is a savage place.
Orpheus:– I cannot recognise this hissing as the voice
          Of my Eurydice.
Eurydice:– Bear in mind, until I leave the darkness
          I am worse than a dragon.
          I will not become my former self until I see
          The blue horizon.
          I will not become my former self until
          My lungs breathe in the painful air.
          I think we're close, I seem to sense
          The wind and the sea.

The voice was a savage gasping,
There was the rustling of a beard.

Orpheus: I am terrified, what if it isn't you, Eurydice,
          I am leading back into the starlight, but…

Plagued by his doubts, he stopped and turned –
A snake with pleading eyes,
Fat as a log, was bustling in his wake;
Terrorstruck, he leapt aside.
From its disgusting belly
Two beloved slender arms with their familiar scar
Stretched out towards him.
Hesitantly he touched the rosy nails.
– No, your heart was blind,
You do not love me, –
Whispered the snake with a bitter smile: –
– Please leave me! please leave me!
And melted like smoke in the shadows of hell.

The Invisible Hunter

Perhaps – to my good fortune or my shame –
My sole worth is nothing but designs
Of birthmarks peppering my skin,
Dark constellations that have forgotten the sky.
The whole thing is a snapshot of the northern night –
Auriga, Aquila, Andromeda, Cygnus,
Spikes and speckles and swarms of dots...
Ah, I dread the way they single me out!
No, it's not my gift, my soul, my voice –
My skin is my most precious attribute,
And a keen-eyed, invisible hunter
May already be on its track.
(Certain whales exist
And there are tortoises
With letters and signs across their backs,
They are slaughtered as curios.)
Perhaps a flautist, a celestial spirit
Had nowhere to write his music
When he woke in eternal night
And in the darkness seized the first white scrap
And scratched his notes into it, jabbed
Snowy, unborn, paper-pale skin...
Perhaps he's searching, will find it, slice it up.
(Do sable, mink or squirrel guess
How many dollars their fur can fetch?)
Though brain will rot and soul fly off,
But skin – no! – that won't give the worms a feast.
For behold, my pegged-out hide
Will be preserved as a palimpsest
Or a photo of the infant heavens.
Where can I hide, where can I run to, what can I do?
I sense keen eyes, hot breath...
Ah, those designs are marked for death.

BORIS SLUTSKY

'Let's meet in hell!'

Let's meet in hell!
I won't have a minute
till death itself,
believe me.

I cannot pick a time.
So come to hell
and come near to the fire –
and let's burn together.

Let's judge our sins
and examine our vices.
Some smart aleck lied
to us about hell

when he said it was chaotic.
On the contrary it is very ordered,
and the law punishes us
with the familiar organs.

We can talk as much as we like,
discuss what we want,
while we burn,
while we burn in the flames.

Doctoring Questionnaires

They lied in the questionnaires,
changed their birth certificates,
feared smoke and fire the same,
and never mentioned the Americas
where their families had emigrated to long ago.

They sheltered their families from unpleasantness,
and forced their simple biographies
closer to the ideal
and trembled slightly and politely.

Yes, the biographies were simple
in all their shameful clarity.
They could be seen from top to toe
without the aid of a spy-glass.

Consciousness reflected existence,
but also deformed and distorted it –
more like the dazzle on a stream, than a mirror,
which honestly fulfils its function.

But who was more to blame:
the stream or the person who looks at the dazzle
and reproaches and despises himself?
I shall tell you about this later.

About the Jews

Jews don't plant wheat
Jews trade in corner-shops
Jews go bald earlier
More Jews are thieves than cops.

Jews are adventurers,
No good at war.
Ivan fights in the trenches.
Abram mans the store.

I've heard it since my childhood.
Soon I'll be decrepit
Still I can't escape it:
The shout of "Jews, Jews".

I've never been in trade.
I've never stolen once.
I carry this damned race
Inside like a disease.

The bullets didn't get me.
This must surely prove
None of the Jews was shot.
They all came home alive.

'I'm not grinding water in water'

I'm not grinding water in water
But translating line by line
As an old man writes,
As an old man breathes,

As an old man falls ill
– Fatally, this time,
As he sums up his whole life
In a single night.

I read about it in books
I saw it on the films
And I refused to accept
That this was my destiny.

But it seems it's mine as well.
Living in misery,
It's as if I'm crawling home
As I reach my familiar old age.

When I was still young
How well-behaved I was.
On the metro I gave up my seat
To the wrinkled and grey-headed.

LARISA VASILIEVA

Recollection

I dreamed of a lost summer,
The swelling noise of rain,
And a poet making jokes
To conceal his idle brain.
A great gift was sold for drink,
And still that gift remained.
He poured away none of his poems,
Though he poured them to the wind.
I inherited his glory
For my loyalty, for my pains.
And all that's left to me now
Is to memorise his lines.

I dreamed of what is lost.
Morning came. And went out.
The poet brightly predicted
Everything, even the date.
But in that prediction I hear,
And can almost see, the echo
Of suffering, ringing clear,
Restoring our sight as we go.

'Thanks'

Thanks. Now I'm able to say
What I want to about the past.
I can make a joke carelessly
Without worrying what it will cost.

Thanks. I can now call a lie,
A lie. "Executioner's Block"
Is a term I can link to real life
And not to the leaves of a book.

Thanks. I can make people listen
with silence, or scare them away
And by a new means of expression
Re-illumine the every-day.

Thanks.
Must I really keep on
Saying thanks for the right to be me?
What's this looming above us again?
Why this weight on our destiny?

ANDREI VOZNESENSKY

Poet to Minister

(Answering a criticism from the poet concerning the overuse of nitrates in fertiliser, N.M. Olshansky, Minister for the Production of Mineral Fertiliser in the USSR, stated that the Danes use 300 kilos of nitrate fertiliser per hectare, whereas the Russians use only 4½ kilos. Voznesensky later found out the true figures: the Danes have 100 times fewer nitrates in their food than the Russians – although, according to the Minister, they use 100 times more!)

Greetings, kind Minister
Of Criminal Fertiliser!
So the Danes eat a hundred times more
Nitrates than we do here?

I'm simply reduced to despair
By the sight of rows of them lying
In the wards of our hospitals
– Danes poisoned, Danes dying!

Don't spray us with pesticide, Minister.
Haven't you ever been woken
By nightmares about the statistics
(Not Danish) of deaths among children?

Help yourself, Minister, please
To the produce our people eat daily.
In Denmark such fruits as these
Are made to retire early.

The Danes suffer great deprivation.
In life's vale of tears they are losers.
They've no Ministry for the Production
Of Mineral Fertilisers.

Abolish your Ministry, Minister!
Put an end to our torment and pains
So that Muscovites, Psokvites and all
Can eat like the miserable Danes!

Candles and Tanks

(in memory of the Georgian Dead)

1

I didn't slaughter those innocents
But they were killed
by my countrymen in my own country
And I'm appalled.

It wasn't in Chile this happened.
My throat's become full.
It must have been tear-gas they used
And it's got to us all.

Pushkin appeared at our meeting *
– The one that was banned.
He moved through the soldiers, shaken,
Top-hat in his hand.

From academicians to first-years,
We're all seeking the laws
Of that gas which can choke perestroika,
And it's looking for us.

And where is the blueprint for rubber
Batons that fly
Against candles? They rest under banners
– Those fated to die.

Candles, run over by tanks
And a child-clear gaze
Will shine in the unquenched souls
Of Georgia, always.

2

I repeat: Pushkin could have been there
At our unauthorised meeting.
Don't hide like a shell-fish behind your umbrella.
It's serious, what I'm saying.

We weren't people, we were ideas.
We'd been too long awaited.
And then, who should turn up
At our unauthorised suicide but hope?

Women, unauthorised too,
Were borne above the streets in coffins.
No singing for them, no cooking the stew,
No washing the children. No children.

The unauthorised sun failed to shine
On the Arbat. Rain fell.
We were snow in the rain, we were the warning-bell.
Massed forces of MVD men
Were waiting for their sign.
Our *unauthorised meeting* wishes
To know what happened, where and when.

And then it dawned on us
– The formula for that gas.
Nobody's lips moved.
Everyone understood.

An unauthorised warning-bell.
– A challenge, like that of the Vendée?**
Unauthorised prayers to a god
Also unauthorised.

Throw the memorial roses to the wind.

Who slaughtered those innocents?
The Saracens? Soaking wet,
We fill the Arbat like tears
Stuck in our country's throat.

* *A meeting on New Arbat, Moscow, to commemorate the dead of Tbilisi. The meeting was not approved by the authorities. Andrei Sakharov and Andrei Voznesensky spoke. Voznesensky's poems had been read at the memorial meeting in Tbilisi.*

** *La Vendée, a coastal area in the West of France, was a centre of resistance to the French Revolution. Savage reprisals against the Vendéans were conducted by the Jacobins.*

Ditch

A Spiritual Process

AFTERWORD

On 7th April 1986 I was driving with some friends along the Feodosia Highway from Simferopol. The clock on the taxi dashboard showed ten in the morning. Vasily Fyodorovich Lesnykh, the driver of our taxi, a man in his sixties, heavy, with a ruddy, windblown complexion, and blue eyes that had faded from what he had seen, kept repeating his harrowing story. Outside the town, here at the 10th kilometre, twelve thousand peaceful inhabitants, for the most part of Jewish nationality, were shot.

'Well, us lads – I was ten then – ran to watch how they were shot. They brought them in covered lorries. They stripped them to their underclothes. There was an anti-tank ditch running from the highway; they just mowed them down with machine gun fire above the ditch. They were all screaming terribly, and their groans hung over the steppe. It was December. They'd all taken off their galoshes and thousands of them were strewn about. Carts were going past on the highway, but the soldiers did not stop them. The soldiers were all drunk. When they saw us they gave us a burst of fire. Oh yes, I remember there was a little table where they collected the passports. Passports were scattered over the whole steppe. Many were buried while still half alive. The earth breathed.

'Later we found a shoe-polish box in the steppe. It was heavy, and in it was a gold chain and two coins, all the family savings. So they'd taken with them all their valuables. Later I heard that someone had discovered this burial place and dug up the gold. They were tried two years ago. But you know about that anyway.'

I not only knew, but had even written a long poem about this that I had called *Avarice,* but that had a latent title *Ditch.* I had interviewed witnesses. People had shown me archive documents. The poem was finished, but wouldn't go out of my mind. I was drawn again and again to the scene of destruction. But what would I see there? Just kilometre after kilometre of overgrown steppe.

'I have a neighbour called Valya Perekhodnik. He was probably the only survivor. His mother pushed him off the lorry as they were being taken there.'

We got out of the car. Vasily Fyodorovich was visibly upset.

A wretched, cracked, once-plastered column with an inscription about the victims of the invaders stood there, and spoke more about oblivion than memorial.

'Shall we take it?' My friend said getting out his camera. The cars streamed down the road. The young shoots of emerald wheat stretched to the horizon. On the left a tiny farm cemetery nestled idyllically on the rise. The ditch was green and had long ago been levelled, but its outline could be seen, coming across from the highway for about one and a half kilometres. Shy branches of blackthorn blossomed white, and the occasional dark acacia stood out.

The sun made us sleepy as we walked slowly down the highway.

Suddenly – what's that? There was a black square of a freshly-dug shaft on the path among the green field; the earth was still damp. Alongside there was another. There were rotten clothes around a mass of charred bones, and smoke-blackened skulls. 'They're digging again, the bastards!' Vasily Fyodorovich had been right.

This was not on documentary film, nor in the stories of witnesses, nor even in a nightmare: it was right here and now. It was all freshly dug up. One skull after another. Two tiny children's ones, and an adult's, smashed into fragments. 'They prise the gold crowns off with pliers, you see.'

A battered woman's shoe. Oh my God, hair and a scalp, a child's red hair in a plait! How tight it was plaited as though they were hoping for something that morning before they were shot...

What bastards! This is not a literary device, these are not heroes that have been dreamed up, or the pages of a criminal investigation – we are standing alongside the busy highway in front of a heap of human skulls. Our people, yes, our people did this, not evil monsters of antiquity. What a nightmare! The bastards were digging last night. A broken filter cigarette is lying on the ground. It's not even damp. Alongside is a brass cigarette case that's turned green. 'German,' Vasily Fyodorovich says. Someone picks it up, but throws it down immediately – there's danger of infection.

The skulls were lying in a heap, those enigmas of creation, dark-brown from long years underground, just like huge smoked mushrooms.

The professionally dug shafts were about twelve feet deep, and in one there was further digging. A shovel with dust on was half-hidden at the bottom of the other. So they're going to come and dig again today!

We looked at each other in horror and disbelief. It was all a terrible dream.

How far can man go, how depraved can his mind be, to dig among skeletons, by the side of a busy road, to crush skulls and prise off crowns with pliers by the light of headlights? And furthermore to conceal virtually nothing and leave everything in evidence so demonstratively, almost as a challenge. As for the people driving calmly down the highway, they would just grin and say: 'Somebody's digging for gold again.' Has everyone gone out of their minds?

There was a tin sign stuck on a stake next to us: 'Digging is prohibited – cable'. So you can't dig up a cable, but you can dig up people? So even the court procedures did not make this bastard stop and think, and as I was told later they only talked at the trial of the perpetrators of the crime and not the fate of those they buried there. And what is the epidemic station doing? All sorts of infections could emerge from those shafts. An epidemic could decimate the region. Children run wild over the steppe. And what about a spiritual epidemic?

They are not robbing graves; the paltry gold grams of base metal are not important; they're robbing souls, the souls of those buried there, our souls, your souls!

The fresh lilies-of-the-valley bloom in the grass. I bend down. It's the bones of a child's little finger, washed clean by last year's rain and floods.

The police patrol the highway for speeders and fines, but do not look over here. They should have a post here. One for twelve thousand. The people's memory is sacred. We should think not only about legal but also spiritual protection of those buried. Just call out and the best sculptors will erect a *stele* or marble plaque, to send a sacred shudder down people's backs.

Twelve thousand are worthy of this. The four of us are standing at the 10th kilometre. We are ashamed and we cannot find the words to express what should be done. Perhaps grass should be laid, and paving stones with a border round. Then names should be remembered. We don't know what should be done, but something should be done fast.

That's how I was confronted with last year's Case No. 1586 which rose again.

Ditch, where are you leading to?

Legend

The Angel of Death comes after your soul,
like a terrible opened-out, three-leaved mirror.
I read in ancient legends
that he is made all of numerous eyes.
Did not Christ or Shestov the philosopher know
why he had such numerous eyes?

If he is mistaken
(for your time is calculated)
he flies away, leaving new sight.
He gives the startled soul
a new pair of eyes.
They say this happened to Dostoyevsky.

You're still on earth,
Valentin Valentin!*
Your mother angel not only saved you,
but gave you the vision of the graves
of twelve thousand pairs of eyes.

And you walk through the plain
with the pain of your new vision.
How your new sight tortures you!
Your breast is not badged with blood
but with the clairvoyant sores of pupils.
And your shirt is rough like haircloth.

You scream in the night,
and see the roots of the cause.
In the morning you look in terror in the triple mirror.
But when that other one
flies in for your soul,
you will not give him your eyes.

Not on the wing of the seraphim,
carried along like a windsurfer
did he cut out and rip out my tongue.
The angel, Valya Perekhodnik*,
drives me without a word
to the Simferopol Ditch.

* *The only survivor of the Ditch (see prose piece)*
  Valya is the diminutive of Valentin

Up the Lighthouse

Like a maniac
I climb the lighthouse.

I go out
onto the platform by the light.
Heat on my back. Midges. Sweat.

My shadow falls from the light
into double clouds of mist and swarming mosquitoes.

My head
lolls in the haze like that of a mutant.
Terrible haze all in my mind.

My bright plans are come from light,
my shaky life comes from the light.

My shadow lies heavy on my soul,
like granite flying from the light.

Light on the subconscious of the sea
and forest,
God and the devil,
on the look cast below.

Ah striped, burning truncheon of God,
point me out the way.

Light, in olden times,
you burned through the mist
saving the caravans of ships with your howl.
Electronic navigation is more convenient now.

But over waters
forests and seas
my shadow still moves from the light.

YEVGENY YEVTUSHENKO

Letter to Yesenin

We Russian poets
          curse one another.
The Russian Parnassus is inhabited by squabbles,
but we are all tied by one thing –
each of us is a bit of a Yesenin.

I am Yesenin
        though someone else entirely.
My rosy steed has been in a Kolkhoz[1] since birth.
I
    like Russia
        am less steely.
I
    like Russia
        am less like a birch-tree.
Dearest Yesenin,
        Russia has changed,
there's no point, I think, in being sorry,
and I'm afraid
        to say it's changed for the better
yet it's dangerous
        to say it's changed for the worse.
What great developments,
        sputniks in our country!
But we have lost, along our bumpy road,
twenty million in the war
and millions
        in the war against the people.
How can we forget this
        without castrating our memory?
But where is the axe
        which castrates memory in one stroke?!
No-one saved others
        like the Russians.

No-one destroyed themselves
                like the Russians.
But our ship's afloat.
                When the water is shallow
we'll drag Russia forward through the dry patches,
and if we've got our share of bastards
                     we can handle them.

We have no Lenin –
               and this is very hard.
And it's a pity
          we don't have you
and your rival with the full throat.[2]
I am not of course the judge of either of you.
Anyway, you both left too early.
When the flushed Komsomol chief
shakes his fists
         at us
            poets
and wants to knead our souls
              like wax,
because he'd like to mould us in his image,
his words, Yesenin, are not frightening,
but you can't be happy about it,
and, believe me,
          I've no wish
             to run
after the Komsomol man,
             wagging my tail.
Sometimes I feel bitter,
        and all this hurts me.
I've no strength to resist the nonsense
and life is drawing me under the wheel
as the scarf once drew Isadora.
But we have to live.
         Neither vodka
             nor the noose

nor women
           are the solution.
Salvation is you,
                      Russian soil,
salvation
           is your sincerity,
                              Yesenin.
And Russian poetry
goes forward
           through suspicion and attack,
and with Yesenin's grasp
puts Europe
           like Podubny[3]
                      on its back.

1. *Collective farm*
2. *Vladimir Mayakovsky, 1983–1930, Soviet poet*
3. *Ivan Podubny, 1871–1949, a famous wrestler*

Monologue of the Day-After-Tomorrow Man

Adam and Eve weren't members of the Party,
the ark was made by non-Party-member, Noah.
All Parties were invented by the devil,
nastily grinning. Devils have no taste.
And maybe sitting deep inside the apple
was politics, the devil's own invention,
worm-like, but not a worm, a snake, in fact,
and people then turned into wormy apples.
Politics created the police-force,
politics created our great leaders,
and termed the living soul a single unit
and split up all the people into Parties.
Where's the Party of widows, cripples, tramps,
where's the Party of families and children?

Where's the border between Maidenek
And Magadan[1], between Songmi[2] and Auschwitz?
Some day, the grandsons of the present time
will remember Parties as a distant age,
a mad, wild Babylon. Oh some day, some day.
The world will be like parkland, green and kindly.
Life for all will be marvellous and simple,
and there'll be one religion and one Party
whose simple name will be – humanity.

1. *Magadan – Siberian town. Symbolic of the Gulag*
2. *Songmi – village in South Vietnam where about 500 people were massacred by American Troops in 1968.*

1972

The Tale of the Turnip

Once we put on a face.
                 Now there's only disgrace.
It's splitting apart,
                 this tumble-down place.
Its walls are propped up
                 by sheiks and sirs.
They feel no pride, being forced volunteers.
Aren't you ashamed
                 oh Soviet state
if drugs have been sent
                 by class enemies, straight
off the front-cover of Krokodil
by ambulance-jet
                 to the babes of Chernobyl?
The story of Lenin's peaked cap
                 is done.

The tale of the turnip
          has once more begun.
To the angry queues
          that's our situation:
we are the turnip
          of all the nations.
They tug us to get us
          out of our jam,
Cowboy-grandad
          and Iron Gran.
They tug us and tug us,
          these foreigners, it's a
mission they have
          – smear our wounds with pizza.
Brighton Beach grand-daughters
                    tug and tug
Luxembourg doggies
                    tug and tug
but we're sunk too deep in the shit, I'm afraid.
The capitalists
          now rush to our aid,
but here we are stuck
          like that turnip-plant.
They tug and they tug and they
          tug – but they can't...

1990

BIOGRAPHIES

Bella Akhmadulina was born in 1937 and graduated from the Literary Institute, Moscow, in 1960. She published her first book in 1955, but her best-known collection of poems is probably *String* (1963). Her other volumes include *Music Lessons* (1969), *Snowstorm* (1977) and *Garden* (1987) her *Selected Poems* were published in 1987. She belongs to the Soviet Writers' Union, is on the executive body of Russian PEN, and is an honorary member of the American Academy of Arts and Letters. She is also a translator, specialising in Georgian. Her first husband, Yevgeny Yevtushenko, described her as the foremost Russian woman poet since Anna Akhmatova. She identifies Marina Tsvetayeva as her chief mentor and forebear.

Nizametdin Akhmetov is a Bashkir Russian poet born in 1949 near the Urals. His family moved to Tashkent in his teenage years, where he became friendly with the Crimean tartars, was involved with various demonstrations and was arrested. This led to his first imprisonment of 20 years. While in prison he became involved in human rights, and began to read and write poetry, making several eloquent appeals to the West in the '70s and '80s. This led to him being transferred to a psychiatric hospital. After a campaign in the West, he was finally freed in 1987 and went to live in Germany.

Gennady Aygi was born in 1934 in the Chuvash Autonomous Republic. He started writing in Chuvash initially, then in Russian, though for more than 20 years not a single book of his was published in Russia itself, and his poems in Russian were brought out in Germany and France and his work widely translated into German, French, Polish and Hungarian. Only now is his work being seen in the USSR, and in 1988 he received the Andrey Beliy Literary Prize for Poetry 'for courageous loneliness in poetic work that has overcome the national limitations of Chuvash, French and Russian and opened up a united field of human culture'. Peter France and Edwin Morgan have translated his work in *Lines* and *Chapman* magazines.

Tatiana Bek was born in Moscow in 1949, is the author of three poetry books in the USSR, and has published many articles on Russian poetry. She is the contemporary poetry consultant for the journal *Druzhda narodov,* and also looks after the literary heritage of her father Aleksandr Bek (1903–72), some of whose work is only recently published in the USSR. Tatiana Bek writes about Moscow, and about love, about her generation, and the dangers of the lack of commitment.

Joseph Brodsky was born in 1940 in Leningrad. He left school at 15 and began writing poetry at 18. From 1964/5 he did hard labour in Archangelsk for 'social parasitism', but did not complete the 5-year sentence. He was forced into exile in 1972 and, after brief stays in Vienna and London, emigrated to the USA where he now lives. His translations of Donne and Milosz appeared in Russia, but almost nothing of his own work, until recently. He was widely published abroad and his volumes of poetry in English include *Selected Poems* (1973), *A Part of Speech* (1980) and *To Urania* (1988). A collection of essays appeared in 1988, *Less than One*. He now has two volumes of poetry published in Russia and another six forthcoming. In 1987 he was awarded the Nobel Prize for Literature. Often elegiac and ironic in tone, his work is characterised by its historical sense, wide-ranging technical mastery and strikingly original diction.

Oleg Chukhontsev was born near Moscow in 1938, and though in 1960 *Sovsky pisatel,* the USSR's largest publishing house, offered to publish his poetry, the book didn't appear for another sixteen years. In 1968 he encountered the anger of the authorities for his poem about Prince Kurbsky, who deserted Ivan the Terrible's Russia for Lithuania, and was unable to publish any of his poetry for several years. He has now published three volumes of verse (*By Wind* and *Ashes* came out in 1989) and is the poetry editor of *Novy Mir.*

Yuri Cobrin belongs to the middle generation of Russian poets, born in 1943 in Siberia, a military family. His early poems were published in Lithuania, which had become his second home, and though he published five poetry collections in Lithuania, it was not until 1987 that his poetry was seen in Moscow: even so his first Russian collection *Diary of Love* excluded twenty poems which, even in the times of glasnost, seemed dangerous to the editor. Working at the junction of two cultures, Cobrin always remembers he is a citizen of Vilnius, and the Lithuanian capital infuses much of his poetry.

Veronica Dolina was born in Moscow in 1956. She writes songs for film and theatre but her main interest is in guitar poetry and, during 1986–1988, she made two records of her songs, *Allow Me to be Faithful* and *My House is Flying*. Her first book of poetry was published in Paris in 1987. In a few years she has become one of the most popular names in the USSR, and in the preface to her latest book *The Aeronaut* she writes, "I am 33 years old, I do not have any major tasks that I would like to fulfil or achieve. I would like to write as far as possible better and better poems and sing. Well, the question is whether it'll turn out that way".

Vladimir Druk was born in 1957 in Moscow, and in 1985 he helped organise the first poetry club of the Moscow cultural underground, including musicians, writers, singers, poets and artists. He was called upon to explain his actions to the KGB. Much of his work has been seen in translation (Germany, France, Denmark, Finland etc) but no collection of his work has so far been published in the USSR. Two of his plays have been performed by Soviet youth theatres. In 1989 he was invited to join the Writers' Union, which he regarded as 'a bastion of conservative corruption'. He finally agreed to join, and fight from inside, by belonging to the April Movement, a splinter group within the Union. His wife, the artist Olga Astafyevna, is leader of the *Narrow School* group of artists, poets, actors and philosophers.

Mikhail Eisenberg, Sergei Gandlevsky, Timur Kibirov, Victor Koval, Denis Novikov and **Dmitri Prigov**, whose ages descend from 45–26, are all members of the Almanac Group based in Moscow, an impressive gathering of avant-garde performance poets who performed at the ICA in London in March of 1988, and who are now beginning to be published in the USSR and abroad.

Sergei Gandlevsky (see Mikhail Eisenberg).

Polina Ivanova is the pseudonym of Olga Yablonskaya. She was born in Moscow in 1964. She participated in a seminar for young poets run by the magazine *Novy Mir* and her first poems were published by the same magazine in 1988. She has also published several poems in the prestigious anthology, *Day of Poetry*. At the moment she is newly married and busy with her family, but she hopes to continue writing poetry in the future. Her work is complex, philosophical and introspective in a manner that suggests Joseph Brodsky's work may be influencing the youngest generations of Russian poets.

Timur Kibirov (see Mikhail Eisenberg).

Oleg Klebnikov was born in 1956 in Izhevsk, near the Urals. His first poems were published in *Komsomolskaya Pravda* when he was 17, and he was soon noticed and praised by Boris Slutsky. After qualifying in mechanical engineering and applied mathematics, he decided to concentrate on poetry and took an advanced course in literature. He has since published five volumes of poetry, including *Letters to Passersby, Town* (a short novel in verse) and *Local Time*. His latest volume, *Street-Level Crossing*, appeared in 1989, and he currently works for the magazine *Ogonyok* in the Department of Literature.

Vladimir Kostrov was born in 1935 in the Kostroma region, graduating in chemistry from Moscow University, and has now published twenty poetry collections. He has a fluent command of several literary genres from civic poetry to the lyrical poem and drama. Kostrov's dramatic poem *Jordano* was turned into a quasi-rock opera, whose final lines by the hero seem to say a great deal about much of Soviet officialdom: "You have to have an ass's patience / to live among asses, not losing face / So many asses – it's a mystery to me. / But the mystery of asses does enrapture me". He is deputy chief editor of *Novy Mir* magazine.

123

Victor Koval (see Mikhail Eisenberg).

Victor Krivulin was born in Leningrad in 1944, the year the siege was lifted. His poetry has its roots in urban folklore, and it includes references to mythology and the great events of history intermingled with the occurrences of everyday life. His work was included in the recent anthology of Eastern European Poetry, *Child of Europe* (Penguin, £6.99), edited by Michael March.

Vyacheslav Kuprianóv was born in 1939 in Novosibirsk. He graduated from the Naval Engineering Academy, Leningrad, in 1960, and the Translation Faculty of the Moscow Institute of Foreign Languages in 1967. His first volume of poems *From the First Person*, was published in 1981. He is unusual among Russian poets in that he works in *vers libre*. He was Laureate of the Poetry Festival, Gonetsa, Italy, in 1986, and has travelled widely for readings and literary festivals. He has published ten books abroad in such countries as Germany, Holland and Sri Lanka, and is a member of the Regensburg International Group in what was West Germany. His most recent collections of poetry are *White Square* (1988) and *Echo* (1989).

Tatiana Kuzovleva is the author of fourteen books of poetry and philosophy. She is a lyrical writer married to the poet Vladimir Saveliev.

Yusus Matzavichus was born in Vilnius, Lithuania, in 1928. He is a poet and editor of the magazine *Victory,* and has published more than twenty books of poetry, and has also written the play *The 20th Century Has Arrived*. His poetry is full of philosophical allegory and aphorisms,.

Yunna Moritz was born in Kiev in 1937. She has published nine books of lyrical poems and six books for children. She has also translated many foreign poets, including Lorca and Seferis, and her work has been translated into English by Elaine Feinstein. Moritz was a member of the Literary Institute in Moscow, from where she was expelled for her anti-Stalinist poems. She also defended Solzhenitsyn.

Olesia Nikolayeva, a Muscovite, represents the middle generation of modern Russian poets. She graduated in 1977 from the Gorky Literary Institute and now lectures in the Institute's Department of Creativity. She is the author of five books of poetry and one of prose. Her verse combines elevated religious tradition with everyday speech. She is studying ancient Greek, plays the piano and sings in the church choir in the Preobrazhensky church in Peredelkino, a writers' village outside Moscow.

Denis Novikov (see Mikhail Eisenberg).

Bulat Okhudzhava was born in 1924, Moscow, of mixed Trans-Caucasian descent. He volunteered for the front in 1942 and studied at the University of Tbilisi after the war. His first collection of poetry, *Lyrics*, was published in 1956. Though a prose-writer as well as poet, it is as a singer-bard that he is best-known. His tapes were widely, but most unofficially, circulated and sung all over Russia. His style is more tender and lyrical than that of the most famous bard of the succeeding generation, Vladimir Vysotsky. He is no longer writing songs, but concentrating on autobiographical essays. His most recent collections of poems are *Dedicated to You* (1988) and *Selected Poems* (1989).

Dmitri Prigov (see Mikhail Eisenberg).

Lev Rubinshtein was born in Moscow in 1947 and represents the so-called 'disorganised culture', which in the '60s and '70s defied the official cultural doctrine and dogmatism. His poems are now being published in Russian and translated into French, Swedish, Finnish, German and (here) English. In the Soviet Union his work is published in the *Teatr, Rodnik* and *Znamya* magazines, a poetry characterised by sharp imagery, interaction and the collision of different rhythms and thematic multi-development. He likes strolling about the town and having lengthy chats and arguments with friends round the table.

Gennady Rusakov was born in 1938 and in 1966 graduated from the First Moscow Institute of Foreign Languages. He now has a perfect command of English, French, Italian and Spanish. He has published four books of poetry and ten books of poetry translation; he compiled and translated a unique volume of the sonnets of Shakespeare's contemporaries which was published in 1987 by the *Kniga* publishing house, and was quickly a best-seller. Rusakov was married to the poet Lyudmila Kopylova, who died in 1990, and his 18 year old poet daughter Maria Rusakov works in the editorial offices of the *Ogonyok* magazine.

Vladimir Saveliev was born in 1934. He studied at the State Literature Institute and has published seventeen books of poetry and one prose book, *The Little Golden Bee*. Saveliev's main direction is romantic realism.

Olga Sedakova was born in Moscow in 1949 and graduated from Moscow State University in 1972, since when she has published translations of such poets as Rilke, Dante, Petrarch, Verlaine, Hardy, and Carroll. She started writing while still at school and published early poems in newspapers for pioneers, and her first book of poems *Friendship of the Peoples* was published in Paris in 1986. Her poems have still not been published in book form in the USSR, but are now appearing more frequently in Soviet literary journals and abroad.

Ekaterina Shevelyova is a Moscovite, poet and prose writer, who represents the older generation of contemporary writers. As she writes "An old inhabitant of a bleak country / Every snowstorm I recall, / Yet a sky track I have made / For the little girl following me". Though she has published 38 books of verse, she has still been unable to get published in the Soviet press her poem about the Warsaw Pact's army's entry into Czechoslovakia (part of which is in this book). She is the compiler and one of the translators of the large collection *Poets of Northern England* published in Moscow in 1988 by Raduga. Her former husband, with whom she maintains a professional relationship, is the well-known writer Alexander Latsis. A fighter by nature, Shevelyova's character was formed during a long and complex life, which included 17 years work at a lathe in the Moscow factory, Dinamo, and journalistic work on a long posting in India.

Elena Shvarts was born in 1948 in Leningrad, where she has since lived. Her first official publication in the USSR was *Storony Sveta* (Leningrad 1989), but during the '70s and '80s she was widely published in samizdat journals and by emigré publishers. In 1989 she took part in an East European poetry festival in London – her first trip abroad. Translations of her work appeared in *Child of Europe* (Penguin 1990, editor Michael March).

Boris Slutsky was born in 1919 and died in 1986. He is arguably one of the outstanding Soviet poets in the second half of the twentieth century and, though he grew up under the banners and trumpets of the October Revolution, and remained faithful to the ideals of the slogans, he retreated further and further from the cruel dogmas which he saw as subjugating a powerful yet unlucky country and millions of human lives. Slutsky, who wrote nineteen books of poems, created verse that portrayed people in their grief and misfortune, and once said, "I shall remain with the weak of the world". In the mid-sixties, he broke forever from the official dogmas, saying, "I have finished dancing your dances, I have finished bathing in your reservoirs".

Larisa Vasilieva is a Moscow poet and prose writer, who began speaking in verse almost as soon as she was aware of the world. She is the author of 30 poetry books, two prose books and many essays and articles. The link with Russian folklore, fairy tales, fantasy and reality is organic to her poetry, which advocates harmonic unity of male and female. In their harmony, which has been disturbed for centuries, lies the salvation of the world. Four women pass through her poetry: mother, daughter, wife and sister; four men watch over her fickleness and contradictoriness: father, son, husband and brother.

Andrei Voznesensky was born in 1933, and came to prominence as a poet in the '60s. His impressive readings in Europe and the USA in the '60s and '70s made him an international figure and his travels and prestige within the USSR allowed him in the '80s to become a spokesman in his poetry for issues from pesticides to anti-Semitism, and to a dynamic exposure of both Stalinism and consumerism.

Yevgeny Yevtushenko was born in 1933 in Siberia, where his Ukrainian grandfather had been exiled. His first volume of poems, *Prospects of the future* appeared in 1952, but it was the long poem *Zima Junction* that first established him as one of the leading poetic voices of the Krushchev thaw. His charisma as a performer, together with his romantic-revolutionary idealism and straightforward literary style, have continued to win him large popular followings, both in the USSR and abroad. He has worked in various media, experimenting with cinema, autobiographical prose, and combinations of poetry-and-prose. Recent volumes available in English translation are *The Poetry of Yevtushenko, The Face Behind the Bars* and *Almost at the End*.

Peter Mortimer, who lives in the North-East coastal village of Cullercoats, is a poet, playwright, critic, and founder editor of IRON Press and Magazine. Nine of his stage plays have been produced, latterly with the Newcastle-based company, Dodgy Clutch (*The Enchanted Pudding*, 1990); *Elvis, Lucy and Captain Sensible* was broadcast on BBC Radio 4 in the same year. Mortimer is the North-East drama critic for *The Guardian*, and his poems include *Utter Nonsense* (IRON Press), *The Shape of Bricks* (Platform Poets) and *To the Magic Castle* (Plain View Press, Texas). *The Last of the Hunters*, a documentary on his six months at sea working with the fishermen of North Shields was published in 1987. His latest book for children, *The Witch and the Maiden* is due from Pivot Press in 1991.

S.J. Litherland is the pen name of Jackie Levitas, former North-East arts journalist. After bringing up a daughter and son in Durham City, where she has lived for 25 years, she went South to study English Literature, first to Ruskin College Oxford, where she got a Distinction, and then to University College London, where she was awarded a First. She is now a free-lance writer and tutor. Publications include: her first collection of poems *The Long Interval* (Bloodaxe 1986); *Modern Poets of Northern England* (anthology, Raduga, Moscow 1988); *Half Light* (collaboration with her daughter, artist Rachel Levitas, launched at the Rebecca Hossack Gallery London 1989); *New Women Poets* (anthology, Bloodaxe Books 1990). Her second collection *Flowers of Fever* is due from IRON Press 1991–2.

Carol Rumens was born in 1944 in London. Her *Selected Poems* and her first novel, *Plato Park,* appeared from Chatto in 1987. She edited Chatto's women's anthology, *Making for the Open* (1985), and has published seven other collections: *A Strange Girl in Bright Colours* (Quartet, 1973); *Unplayed Music* (1981) and *Star Whisper* (1983) from Secker; *Direct Dialling* (1985) and *From Berlin to Heaven* (1989) from Chatto; and *Scenes from a Gingerbread House* (1982) and *The Greening of the Snow Beach* (1988) from Bloodaxe. Her first play, *Nearly Siberia,* was premiered by Pascal Theatre Company in 1989. She is an occasional translator of Russian poetry, and has a small group of translations in Ratushinskaya's collection *Pencil Letter* (Bloodaxe, 1988). *The Greening of the Snow Beach* (Poetry Book Society Recommendation) includes some of her translations of Blok and Mandelstam. From 1988 to 1990 she was Northern Arts Literary Fellow at the Universities of Durham and Newcastle. She is a freelance writer, and lives in London.

Richard McKane is a London based translator whose previous work includes: *Anna Akhmatova Selected Poems* (Bloodaxe Books, 1989), poems in the two anthologies *Penguin Post War Russian Poetry 1973* (reissuing) and *The Penguin Book of Turkish Verse 1976;* editor and translator, *20th Century Russian Poetry,* (Kozmik Press); *Nazim Hikmet, A Sad State of Freedom* with Taner Baybars (1990 Greville Press Pamphlet); *Osip Mandelstam The Moscow Notebooks,* Richard and Elizabeth McKane (Bloodaxe Books, 1990); *Victoria Andreyeva* (Russian and English) *Dream of the Firmament* (Gnosis Press, New York, and Diamond Press, London) and from the same publisher, *Poems of Leonid Aranzon* (Russian and English). His own verse has been published as *The Rose of the World and Poems 1967–1989* (Gnosis and Diamond Press). Weidenfeld and Nicolson are to publish in 1991 his translations of the poetry and prose of Andrei Voznesensky.

IRON Press was formed in Spring 1973, initially to publish the magazine IRON which almost two decades, and more than 1,000 writers on, survives as one of the country's most active alternative mags – a fervent purveyor of new poetry, fiction and graphics. £8.00 gets you a subscription. Try our intriguing book list too, titles which can rarely be found on the shelves of mega-stores. Fortified by a belief in good writing, as against literary competitions or marketing trivia, IRON remains defiantly a small press. Our address is on page 2.